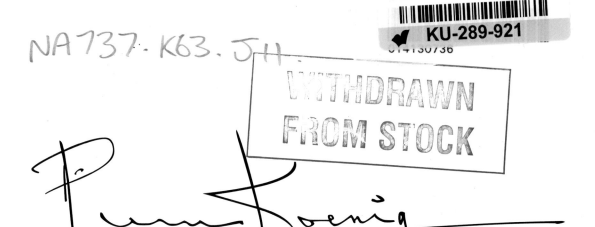

7 DAY LOAN

THE UNIVERSITY OF LIVERPOOL
SYDNEY JONES LIBRARY
RESTRICTED LOAN

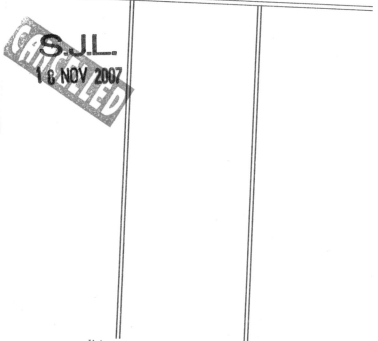

...onditions of borrowing, see Library Regulations

Neil Jackson

PIERRE KOENIG

1925–2004

Living with Steel

TASCHEN

HONG KONG KÖLN LONDON LOS ANGELES MADRID PARIS TOKYO

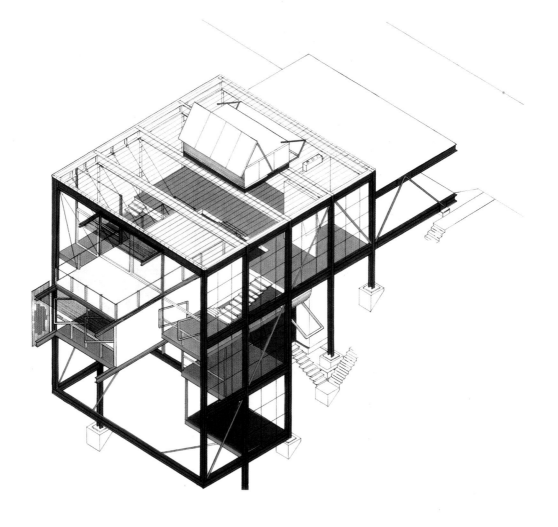

Illustration page 2 ▶ Pierre Koenig at the Bailey
House, 1959
Illustration page 4 ▶ Laguna House, axonometric

© 2007 TASCHEN GmbH
Hohenzollernring 53, D-50672 Köln
www.taschen.com

Editor ▶ Peter Gössel, Bremen
Project management ▶ Katrin Schumann, Bremen
Design and layout ▶ Gössel und Partner, Bremen
Text edited by ▶ Christiane Blass, Cologne

Printed in Germany
ISBN-978-3-8228-4891-3

To stay informed about upcoming TASCHEN
titles, please request our magazine at
www.taschen.com/magazine or write to
TASCHEN America, 6671 Sunset Boulevard,
Suite 1508, USA-Los Angeles, CA 90028,
contact-us@taschen.com, Fax: +1-323-463.4442.
We will be happy to send you a free copy of
our magazine which is filled with information
about all of our books.

Contents

6 Introduction

16 Koenig House #1
20 Lamel House
26 Bailey House (Case Study House #21)
34 Seidel House
42 Stahl House (Case Study House #22)
50 Johnson House
56 Oberman House
62 Iwata House
66 Beagles House
70 Chemehuevi Prefabricated Housing Tract
74 Burton Pole-House
76 Gantert House
80 Koenig House #2
86 Schwartz House

92 Life and Work
95 Map
96 Bibliography / The Author / Credits

Introduction

Few images of twentieth-century architecture are more iconic than the nighttime view of Pierre Koenig's Case Study House #22 set on its eagle's-nest site high above the lights of Los Angeles. Yet neither the house, nor the photograph which captured it, were in fact as they appear. The house was unfinished and full of plaster dust, the furniture, including Koenig's own architectural pottery, was borrowed for the day, and the landscaping was contrived, consisting of cut branches held by clamps or by hand. The photograph was also a construct, a seven-minute exposure to bring out the city lights and the pop of a flash-bulb to catch the two young women, one a UCLA undergraduate and the other a senior at Pasadena High School, poised in conversation inside; in fact, the city lights can actually be read through their white evening dresses. But the picture which first appeared on the front cover of the 'Sunday Pictorial' section of the *Los Angeles Examiner* on 17 July 1960 was symbolic. Like so much popular music, it caught the spirit of the moment, the zeitgeist: Los Angeles, the city of angels at the dawn of the 1960s and the Kennedy era. It was a decade which, for America, started with so much hope but ended in so much chaos. Perhaps that is the lasting significance of this house; it is an enduring statement of hope and expectation.

Pierre Koenig was born in San Francisco on 17 October 1925; his parents were both second-generation immigrants, his mother of French descent and his father of German, hence the European name. In 1939, while still at high school, he moved with his family to Los Angeles, to the San Gabriel valley just south of Pasadena, where he found everything, in contrast to San Francisco, to be "warm, sunny and colourful ... new and bright and clean, especially the architecture".[1] Soon after, in 1941, the United States entered the War and Koenig, then aged just seventeen, enlisted in the US Army Advanced Special Training Program, which promised an accelerated college education. But in 1943, after just a few months at the University of Utah, the programme was cancelled and Koenig was sent to Infantry School at Fort Benning, Georgia. Active service in France and Germany—as a flash ranging observer with the duty to spot enemy gunfire and calculate, through triangulation, their position—kept him in Europe until well after VE Day, and it was not until 1946 that he was shipped back to the United States on the Cunard Liner Queen Mary. On that journey he shunned the squalor of the troops' quarters below decks for a bed-roll in a lifeboat.

The GI Bill granted Koenig the financial support to undertake college training and, after two years at Pasadena City College, he finally gained admittance to the architecture programme at the University of Southern California. Although progressive in many ways, the programme's adherence to timber framing frustrated Koenig, and as a third-year student he proceeded to build his first house using the industrial material steel. "It occurred to me," he later recalled, "that houses that were very slender were meant to be in steel, not wood."[2] It was not surprising then, that rather than seeking work with Richard Neutra, at that time probably the doyen of southern California architects, Koenig should turn instead to another USC graduate, Raphael Soriano. As he later said, "I needed a summer job so I naturally went to him. And because I had

1 Pierre Koenig, quoted in James Steele and
David Jenkins, *Pierre Koenig*, Phaidon Press,
London, 1998, p. 9

2 Ibid., p. 11

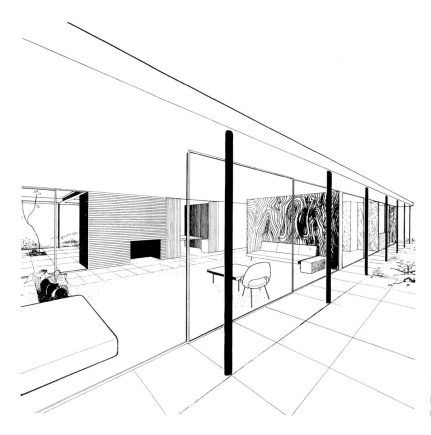

Left and below:
**Pierre Koenig's perspective drawings of
Raphael Soriano's Case Study House 1950**

something to offer him and he to me, I worked for him for that summer."[3] It was a mutually beneficial arrangement.

In that summer of 1950, while Koenig was building his own house in Glendale, Soriano had four lightweight steel-framed houses underway on site or in the design stage: the Shulman House and the Curtis House were almost complete, and the Olds House and the Krause House were in process. Here Koenig recognised a rational, industrial architecture which reflected his own beliefs and thus confirmed, for him, the correctness of his direction. Soriano's drawings, often in crayon and pencil, rarely caught the crispness which so characterised these buildings, so Koenig prepared for him the perspective drawings of the Olds House which were published in John Entenza's magazine *Arts & Architecture* that August as the Case Study House for 1950. Even at this early stage, Koenig's drawings are instantly recognisable. Constructed in black line and two-point perspective, they are as spare and brittle as the houses they portrayed.

The Case Study House Program was the single most significant initiative in post-war Californian architecture and had world-wide influence. John Entenza, who later became director of the Graham Foundation in Chicago, used the magazine *Arts & Architecture*, of which he was both proprietor and editor, to promote a modern, affordable architecture for the post-war years. By publishing selected houses month by month, as they were being designed and then built, he provided publicity for the architect and advertising for the contractors and manufacturers. The benefit to the client was that the materials were supplied at a substantially reduced cost but, in return, the clients had to open their houses to the public for viewing. The houses were not

3 Pierre Koenig interviewed by Neil Jackson, 13 July 1988

ommissioned by the magazine, but selected by Entenza. As Koenig later said, "John ntenza asked me to come in one day and he said to me, 'Pierre, if you ever have a ,ood house with some good clients tell me and we'll make it a Case Study House'. Well did and that was Case Study House 21."[4]

With his two Case Study Houses, Koenig completed the run of eight steel-framed uildings which, in a period of just over ten years, gave the Case Study House Program ts reputation. First was the Eames House (CSH#8), by Charles and Ray Eames, and hen its neighbour, the Entenza House (CSH#9) by Charles Eames and Eero Saarinen. They were both completed in 1949. Soriano's Olds House was the Case Study House or 1950. The next three were by Craig Ellwood: the Salzman House (CSH#16) in 1953, he Hoffman House (CSH#17) in 1956,and the Fields House (CSH#18) in 1958. Case study House #21 was opened to the public is January of the following year and then, as Koenig recalled, "John said we'll do another one. We did Case Study House #22, which s on a eagle's-nest site in the Hollywood hills."[5]

The Case Study House Program promised so much but ultimately it delivered so ittle: it was, as Peter Reyner Banham wrote in *Los Angeles, The Architecture of Four Ecologies*, 'The Style That Nearly ...' But Koenig was not interested in style. That his architecture is seen as having a recognisable style was the result of his rational single-mindedness and the product of later critical readings. When he built his first house in Glendale, he was simply following what he thought was a logical course. As he later said, "This was the same time Charles Eames was doing his building in the Palisades and the same time, so far as I know, Mies was doing Farnsworth House. And none of us, I think, had any inkling of what the other was doing."[6] Looking back thirty years later, Koenig recalled the feelings of the time. "A lot of things went on in Los Angeles that were not really considered to be of any great significance in terms of art or archi-tecture in the world. Music that same way. The fact that Stravinsky and Schoenberg had played here and were having concerts at UCLA was of no great significance. Nothing was going on here that was of any great significance until now—now we look back and we see all these things being important. But you have to understand that at the time there was great excitement, the war was over, everybody was very idealistic. Everybody wanted to produce answers to housing problems. Everybody was going into mass pro-duction, systems, social problems were being addressed. It was an exciting period of time and all kinds of things were being tried."[7]

Music—or sound—was, for Koenig, part of his development. The war had left its memories. In 1999 he confided to Steve Roden that he had "just purchased the engine sounds of a Messerschmitt 109G which produces the most awesome man-made noise in the world. There are two overlapping major elements, a very, very ear-splitting roar with a high-frequency nasty tappet overlay. Distinguishable from any other aircraft in the world. Combine that with the sound of machine guns firing and you have the ultimate psychological effect not easily forgotten."[8] More peacefully, he had discovered music when, as a fourteen-year-old, he heard Igor Stravinsky's *Rite of Spring* on the radio. "The more I listened to music, the more I wanted the newer stuff."[9] In the end his music collection numbered almost 6,000 records, and the music room was as important to his new house in Brentwood, Los Angeles, as were the acoustics of the atrium space where he would play it.

When in 1958 Koenig built a radio station for KYOR in Blythe, California, he demon-strated an early understanding not just of acoustics, but also of flexible system

4 Ibid.
5 Ibid.
6 Ibid.
7 Ibid.
8 Pierre Koenig interviewed by Steve Roden, in Brandon LaBelle and Steve Roden [eds], *Site of Sound: of Architecture & the Ear*, Errant Bodies Press, Los Angeles, 1999, p. 130
9 Ibid., p. 128

building: here the floor deck was raised and could be removed for the routing and rerouting of cables. Designed with a steel frame between concrete block sidewalls, it combined an uninterrupted, multi-purpose rentable ground-floor space with the radio station above. On the front elevation, the glazed lower floor contrasted with the smoothly rendered façade above, thus declaring the privacy and acoustic isolation of the broadcasting studio and control room within.

Koenig's structural engineer on the KYOR radio station building was William Porush, who was to work with Koenig on all his completed buildings, from the first house in Glendale through to the West House at Vallejo, near San Francisco, in 1970. Thereafter, his position was briefly taken by Tom Harris for the Burton Pole-House at Malibu, and then for the next ten years by Dimitry Vergun. Only in the last two or three years did he use other engineers: Norman Epstein for the addition to his neighbour Jeffrey Ressner's house on Dorothy Street in Brentwood; Ficcadenti & Waggoner for the LaFetra House and the Koppany Pool House; and Rubicon Engineering for the Tarassoly & Mehran House. From the beginning, Porush, whom Koenig readily credited when the buildings were eventually published, facilitated his ideas and enabled him to work far beyond the confines of the steel and glass domestic architecture for which he is largely remembered. As he said, "I'm always trying new materials."[10] The Seidel Beach House, built in 1961 at Malibu, was, like the later Burton Pole-House, a timber-frame building which used steel cross-bracing rods to stabilise the structure. The mobile exhibition pavilion built the next year for Bethlehem Steel was of steel and timber and was designed for easy assembly and dismantling. It travelled the United

Radio Station KYOR, Blythe, California, 1958

10 Pierre Koenig interviewed by Neil Jackson,
    13 July 1988

Bethlehem Steel exhibition pavilion, 1962

Seidel Beach House, Malibu, California, 1961

States for two years and, in 1964, won an award in Portland, Oregon, for Best Exhibition Building. The Mosque, commissioned in 1963 by the Moslem Association of America for a site in Hollywood, was to have a prefabricated pre-stressed concrete frame with brick infill walls. This would have been Koenig's only concrete-frame building, but it was never built. The Electronic Enclosures Incorporated Factory and Showroom at El Segundo, built in 1966 on a scale hitherto not attempted, used long-span open-web trusses to provide a column-free internal space with tilt-up concrete panels and glazed walls to enclose it. And then, for the West House Koenig specified Corten, a steel that rusts. Built as the first of a speculative, modernist development, it promised a great opportunity for Koenig to exploit his interest in prefabrication and multiple unit design, but the client died before the house could be occupied and the development was never begun.

Although he worked largely as a sole practitioner, Koenig's architecture was not created in a vacuum but through the learning environment of a school of architecture. Since 1961, he had taught at the University of Southern California, becoming an Assistant Professor in 1964 and an Associate Professor with tenure in 1968. Surprisingly he had to wait until 1996 to become a full Professor, although only three years later he was elected by the University as its Distinguished Professor of Architecture. During that time, from 1969 to 1972, he had been Assistant Director under Konrad Wachsmann of the Institute of Building Research, and from 1971 to 1976, Director of the Comprehensive Planning Program for the Chemehuevi Indian Reservation, an initiative which began as a student project within the School. In 1983 Koenig became Director of the

Electronics Enclosures Incorporated Factory
and Showroom, El Segundo, California, 1966

Building Research Program, which allowed him to pursue research into what he called Natural Forces Response—the effects of gravity, sun, water and wind on architecture. Central to this was the wind tunnel, which enabled him to investigate air movement in contexts as divergent as urban landscapes or single-room apartments. It was through this facility that he developed the working model for his own house in Brentwood, which clearly demonstrated his attitude towards ventilation. "It's essential that we be able to cool our buildings with natural means. I have no artificial air conditioning in any of my buildings in the Los Angeles basin. With the possible exception of the Colorado River, where the temperatures reach 124 °F, there's absolutely no justification to have artificial cooling in a building in southern California as long as you have access to the ocean breeze which is throughout the basin, with the exception of San Fernando Valley and some other valleys."[11]

An equal awareness of passive solar gain is apparent throughout his architecture, from the broad, overhanging eaves of Case Study House #22 to the vertical fins which shelter the Iwata House. But these were fixed devices. In the last building Koenig supervised on site, a small pool house built for Bill and Cindy Koppany, he introduced tilting panels that could be angled to follow the path of the sun. Completed posthumously in 2006 by his colleague and assistant Jan Ipach, it stands in the grounds of a house by Gregory Ain located just beyond the Hollywood Freeway in the East Hollywood hills. Set on a north/south axis parallel to the lap pool, the pool house is a simple

11 Jackson interview, ibid.

Design for a Mosque, Hollywood, California, 1963

steel pavilion of three bays, each 10x12 cm with a west-facing sliding glazed wall to the pool. The flat roof extends almost 3 feet 4 inches beyond the glazed wall towards three 10x10 foot pivoting canvas screens, which provide shelter, when horizontal, from the midday sun and, when vertical, from the evening sun. Thus when the glazed wall is withdrawn, and the canvas screens horizontal, the building offers a sheltered, ventilated space above the pool which, as the sun moves across the sky, the horizontal canvas screens allow for self-adjustment.

The often empirical nature of Koenig's architecture never allowed him to become commercially attractive. When asked in 1971 why the factory-made house, such as he and Konrad Wachsmann were promoting, was not accepted by the house-building industry, he replied: "Prejudice and tradition ... The lady of the house has been brought up to have a set image in her mind of what a dream house should look like. The developer plays on these deep emotional drives, he advertises the selling points, the style, the surface."[12] There were times, in the late-1960s and mid-1970s, when so little finished work was emanating from the office that his major efforts must have been directed to his teaching. This was particularly noticeable between 1986 and 1993, when the architectural fashion for Post-Modernism left Koenig very much out in the cold. But fashions change and his last few years were some of his busiest. When Billy Rose was pressing him for a quick response regarding the restoration of the Gantert House in 2003, Koenig replied: "Sorry I took so long to answer your e-mail. Tell your partners

12 Pierre Koenig quoted in Doug Shuit, 'Lab may brew up your new home', *Los Angeles Times*, 12 December 1971, section F, p. 3

LaFetra House, Malibu, California, 2003
Perspective computer rendering

they can have the plans: 1. Quick, 2. Good or 3. Inexpensive. They can have any 2 out but not all three."[13]

Koenig never had the opportunity to see the completion of the Gantert House restoration nor of his last two buildings, the LaFetra House and the Tarassoly & Mehran House. Although both these new houses were to be located in Malibu, they could hardly have been more different. One was to be a crisp, contained box on a rocky foreshore, while the other was designed as a series of stepped pavilions on a canyon hillside. Koenig's death from leukaemia on 4 April 2004 might have brought a halt to these two schemes had he not nominated James Tyler to take on the work. Jim Tyler had been an Associate in Craig Ellwood Associates between 1965 and 1977, since when he has been in private practice. It was Tyler who was responsible for much of the design work that emanated from Ellwood's office in the later years, and he is now recognised as the author of the Arts Centre College of Design in Pasadena (1970–1976). He had been a colleague of Koenig's in the School of Architecture at the University of Southern California and understood Koenig's architecture and his use of materials, so the choice was not surprising. But for Tyler it was unexpected; it was Koenig's widow Gloria who told him of her late husband's wish and who sent Michael LaFetra to see him. Tyler's completion of the LaFetra House will inevitably leave the impress of his own hand, for many details were still unresolved when Koenig died. At the LaFetra House, for example, a way had to be found to safeguard the exposed steel from the corrosive effects of the salt-air environment. "My hope," Tyler has said, "is that Michael will get a very good house—a Pierre Koenig House, executed as well as it can be."[14] This would further be achieved by the retention of Joe Bavaro of the Bavaro Design Studio for the interior design, because Bavaro had previously worked with Koenig on the Rollés' second addition to the Seidel House (1994) and on the Schwartz House (1996). And the same sense of responsibility to the original intent has been demonstrated by Vida Tarassoly: "The house shall be true to Pierre's signature design and he wanted us to use Jim for the completion of the project. We have talked to Jim and are planning to use his services during construction."[15]

With the exception of one or two fallow periods, Koenig received a constant stream of architectural awards throughout his professional life. In 1957, the year he qualified to practise as an architect, he received the São Paolo Biennale Exhibition Award, an AIA *House and Home* magazine Award, and the Architectural League of New York Award. The following year, soon after his thirty-third birthday, he completed his first Case Study House, which won him two further awards in 1959 and yet two more in 2000, following its restoration. By then both that house, and Case Study House #22, had been designated Historical Cultural Monuments by the Los Angeles Conservancy. In 1967 the Oberman House was named by the American Institute of Architects (AIA) Southern California Chapter as one of the best 36 houses built since 1947, a recognition which no doubt helped him secure a tenured position at the University of Southern California the following year. In 1971, aged only forty-five, he was admitted to the College of Fellows of the AIA at an investiture ceremony held at the Detroit Institute of Arts. But it was not until he was almost in his sixties, the age when most people begin to think of retirement, that the more hyperbolic awards began to arrive. There was the AIA Olympic Architect Award in 1984; the Los Angeles Department of Cultural Affairs Award in 1989; the AIA California Council 25 Year Award and the Maybeck Award for Lifetime Achievement, both in 1996; and the AIA Los Angeles Chapter Gold Medal a

13 E-mail from Pierre Koenig to Billy Rose, no date
14 James Tyler quoted in: Eryn Brown, 'A Case Study in Stewardship', *Los Angeles Times*, 4 August 2005, p. 10
15 Vida Tarassoly, e-mail to Neil Jackson, 23 July 2006

Tarassoly & Mehran House, Malibu, California, 2003
Perspective computer rendering

well as the Pacific Design Center Star of Design for Lifetime Achievement in Architecture, in 1999. Yet for all this glitter, Koenig had not received, since 1957, a foreign award until, following a change in the rules for qualification, the Royal Institute of British Architects made him an Honorary Fellow in 2000. The ceremony was held in London at Inigo Jones's Banqueting House in Whitehall but, sadly for Koenig, he was unable to attend.[16]

The obituaries which followed Koenig's death appeared world-wide. This was a confirmation of his considerable reputation. At home, the *Los Angeles Times* described his houses as "progressive symbols of postwar suburbia"[17] and acknowledged him as "a key figure in a generation that helped make Los Angeles one of the great laboratories of 20th century architecture. Of these visionaries," it continued, "Koenig seemed best able to capture the hopes and anxieties of California's booming middle class."[18] Sylvia Lavin, Chair of the Department of Architecture and Urban Planning at the University of California, Los Angeles, commented that these architects were trying to create a way of life in which they believed. "It was really a calling," she said. "With Koenig, part of the evidence is that he stayed the course, even when it was no longer fashionable."[19] But Koenig stayed the course only because he recognised imperatives other than style, such as the need for industrialisation and prefabrication and the importance of sustainability. In both fields, he was ahead of his time. Industrialisation and prefabrication are still for many architects a dream and for the domestic building industry a nightmare. But they will catch up. Sustainability, characterised by Koenig's insistent use of natural ventilation, is now being taken more seriously by many individuals and by some governments. Yet he remained jaundiced in his view: "Nobody seemed interested at the time, and they still aren't."[20] In many ways the problem lay in the society he served, for the ephemerality of Los Angeles is at once both its attraction and its undoing. Only here could Case Study House #22 be better known by most people from Julius Shulman's seven-minute image than from Koenig's material architecture.

In summarising Koenig's life for *The Architects' Journal*, David Jenkins wrote: "Watching the pendulum swing towards a renewed understanding of social and environmental concerns, one sees Koenig's work as providing a beacon for younger architects, something that would surely have surprised this unfailingly modest man."[21] In the difficult world of architecture, that is an achievement of which Koenig could have been justly proud.

16 Koenig's Hon FRIBA was received in his absence by Neil Jackson.
17 'Pierre Koenig Dies', *Los Angeles Times*, 6 April 2004, p. 1
18 Nicolai Ouroussoff, 'Pierre Koenig, 78; Architect's Designs Personify Modernism', *Los Angeles Times*, 6 April 2004, p. B11
19 Sylvia Lavin quoted in Ouroussoff, p. B11
20 Christopher Reed, 'Pierre Koenig', *The Independent*, 2004
21 David Jenkins, 'Pierre Koenig (1925–2004)', *The Architects' Journal*, 15 April 2004, p. 12

1950 ▸ Koenig House #1
2002 Los Encinos Avenue, Glendale, California

Opposite page:
Dining and living area, with view through to
the patio

Modular components make up the street
façade.

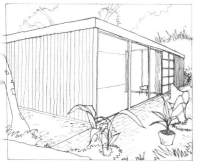

Perspective drawing of garden front

Koenig built this 1000-square-foot house for himself while in his penultimate year of studies at the University of California. His interest in steel as a material for domestic architecture had emerged in the design studio despite the reservations of his tutors. Their scepticism was because they saw steel as an industrial material less suited than timber to domestic construction. In choosing to build with steel, Koenig was, like Raphael Soriano and Charles and Ray Eames, breaking new ground and transferring the technology of the factory to the domestic stage. "I was too innocent then," he later told Esther McCoy, then writing for the *Los Angeles Times Home Magazine*, "to know that it was different. But that has an advantage. When you're too young to distinguish between the possible and the impossible, you often accomplish more." The initial design had been both naive and wasteful. But following discussions with product representatives, he succeeded in rationalising the design and reducing the cost from the first $12,000 estimate to the $5,000 budget figure which allowed him to build it.

Mindful now of the need for modular planning and the use of standardised materials, he designed the house on a square 10-foot grid. The domestic accommodation was arranged as a 40x20-foot enclosed rectangle with the 10x20-foot open carport attached to form an L-shaped plan. The frame was constructed of 3.5-inch concrete-filled pipe columns (known as lally columns), C-section edge beams and a central I-beam. Flanking the east end of the house and the adjacent carport, Koenig built a concrete block retaining wall which provided lateral stability for the frame, and at the other end he closed off the space with vertically hung steel cladding, insulated with cork and finished internally with beech-ply. The long side walls were enclosed with 4-foot-wide units of factory sash windows and a single 20-foot sliding glass door which opened to the south-facing patio at the rear.

Below:
Plan, with the carport and entranceway defined by the columns and roof above

This sense of openness pervaded the building, from the carport and entranceway to the galley kitchen and sliding screens which separated the sleeping area from the living area. The grey painted steel decking provided, from one end of the house to the other, a continuous ceiling plane uninterrupted by partition walls. Within this apparently single volume, the regular grid of columns defined the entranceway, the kitchen, sleeping and bathroom areas, while in the living area, Koenig removed the central column to create a 20x20-foot volume. As a result, the central I-section beam was exposed but rather than awkwardly sub-divide the room, it served to suggest a separation between the sitting area, facing onto the rear patio, and the generous circulation space linking the kitchen and entranceway, in which Koenig placed his drawing board.

The choice of a 10-foot module allowed for the most economical use of standard factory-made components—sash windows and corrugated steel decking. Surprisingly, the single 20-foot sliding glass door to the rear patio proved to be half the cost of the

View from the living area towards the kitchen and sleeping area

The kitchen with the carport beyond

two 10-foot sliding glass doors Koenig had proposed to use. Koenig contracted out the erection of the frame, which took two days, as well as the laying of the concrete slab and the installation of the services, but did much of the semi-skilled labour himself, the final cost being about $10/square foot. It had cost him no more than a timber frame house built under similar conditions would have done and won him an Award of Merit from *House and Home* magazine.

The success of the house can be judged by the readiness with which the steel industry took it up as an advertising model. In 1956 the National Steel Corporation of Pittsburgh featured the house in two-page advertisements in both *Time* and *Newsweek* magazines: "The home is light and spacious," it quoted Koenig as saying, "with all the strength, durability, warmth, beauty and economy desired for modern living. And *steel* makes this possible." Pictured under the heading, 'I built this house of steel for many reasons ...', the house appeared to be less of an advertisement than a manifesto.

1953 · Lamel House
1884 Los Encinos Avenue, Glendale, California

Opposite page:

Entrance patio with living and dining areas beyond

With the exception of the two Case Study Houses, the small house which Koenig designed for Jacqueline and Edward Lamel in Glendale in 1953 gave him more publicity than any other early building. *Arts & Architecture* first carried drawings of the building in January 1954, noting that "the structure is all steel frame." Almost eighteen months later, in June 1955, the magazine published the house again, showing photographs of the completed building and once more emphasising its construction: "Steel is used in the construction in such a way as to achieve maximum use and economy." Considering that Koenig himself would have provided the description, if not the actual copy, it is clear that the use of steel was seen as being significant. Its novelty was not wasted on the popular press, who were quick to use the Lamel House, together with houses by Raphael Soriano, Archibald Quincy Jones and others, to make the point. Under the headline 'There May Be a Steel House ... In Your Very Near Future', Barbara East wrote in the *San Francisco Examiner* that September that, "As a material steel is about as American as apple pie." In February 1956 Esther McCoy wrote in the *Los Angeles Examiner*, *Pictorial Living* of the international appeal of steel house construction, linking the Lamel House with other houses in Mexico and Australia: "It's neutral, but not cold, says Koenig of steel, pointing out that it's a means to open our houses to wooded sites and to bring sun into intimate patios." In the same month, the New York-based magazine *Living For Young Homemakers* featured the house, while referring to Koenig as an architect, an indiscretion which elicited from Koenig a hasty telegram to the editor, Edith Evans, dated 23 January 1956: "Many thanks for fine article on Lamel House. May I correct two errors? I am not a licensed architect. House cost $12,000 without owner's work."

The protection of title which the architectural licence afforded was something of which Koenig was mindful. In October 1957 the California State Board of Examiners granted him "the right to practice architecture and to use the title Architect" and on 23 December that year he was elected a member of the AIA, with election to the Southern California Chapter following the next February. In July 1957, Esther McCoy, writing now for the *Los Angeles Times*, had been careful not to refer to Koenig as an architect although the article was entitled, 'What I Believe ... A statement of architectural principles by Pierre Koenig.' Using the Lamel House as an illustration, she tells readers that "Koenig prefers exposing the structure because it reduces cost and is also aesthetically acceptable." And again she quotes him: "Good living arrangement does not come from steel construction, but this material makes better solutions possible." By the time the house was featured as 'Home of the Week' in the *Independent Star-News* in August 1958, it was hardly new, but it was the first time Koenig could show a completed building and promote his title. "Despite its steel and glass construction," Margaret Stovall wrote, "there is nothing cold and uninviting about the contemporary home designed by Architect Pierre Koenig, AIA ..."

This record of publications is worth reiterating for it shows, in a sense, Koenig's coming of age. No longer was he a young designer building a steel-frame house for

Framed and screened patios allow the house
to merge with the landscape

Right:
Plan, showing how the house integrates with
the landscape.

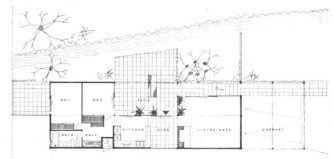

imself, but now he was a qualified architect with a published philosophy and a client ecord to his name. The articles in newspapers and the popular press were, in a way, nore important than those in the architectural press, for they served to advertise 'oenig's skill to potential clients rather than promote his philosophy to his peers. Thus 'unset magazine's small piece on the Lamel House in April 1959 was as valuable as any •f the advertisements in the architectural journals paid for by United States Steel, or he article in the September 1957 issue of L'Architecture d'aujourd'hui which featured ne Lamel House.

The house which had drawn all this attention was only 1,000 square feet in area, but :s linear plan and its heavily planted site made it interesting. The steel frame, 80x20 feet,

The house is cut into and placed above the slope to allow access to and privacy from the road.

RESIDENCE FOR MRS & MRS LEMAL
PIERRE KOENIG
2002 LOS ENCINOS AVE. GLENDALE CALIF. CL 15615

Exterior and interior perspective drawings

adopted the same technology and modular scale as Koenig's own house further down the same block. The sloping site allowed for a carport to protrude from one end at a lower level and at the main level, the 10 feet grid enabled Koenig to open up the plan to introduce a patio within the curtilage of the frame, thus confusing the distinction between indoor and outdoor space. This, combined with the natural canopy of the oak trees which covered the site, extended the sense of enclosure far beyond the normal domestic confines. As the 'Home of the Week', Margaret Stovall promoted the openness of its plan: "The 1,000-square-foot structure fits into its oak-studded site with all the adaptability of a log cabin, providing an indoor-outdoor way of life its pioneer ancestor could never have achieved." But for Koenig, there was nothing novel in this

The patio from the bedroom

"The steel house is considered new," he told Esther McCoy in his statement of principles, "although it's been with us for three decades ... The steel house is out of the pioneering stage, but radically new technologies are long past due. Any large-scale experiment of this nature must be conducted by industry, for the architect cannot afford it. Once it is undertaken, the steel house will cost less than the wood house. The architects have carried the ball a long time and now it's industry's turn." Yet there was a reluctance within the building industry to take the idea further and it fell to enthusiasts such as John Entenza to take up the challenge.

1956–1958 ▸ Bailey House

Case Study House #21
9038 Wonderland Park Avenue, Los Angeles, California

opposite page:
ew from the carport showing the
insparency and regularity of the design

e Case Study House from the road

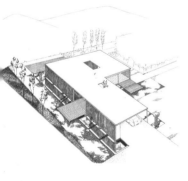

rial perspective showing how the house
egrates with the landscape

Koenig had first become involved in *Arts & Architecture's* Case Study House Program when he had worked for Raphael Soriano and drawn perspectives of the Case Study House for 1950. His own house in Glendale was published by the magazine three years later. As he said of Soriano, they both had something to offer each other and it was probably the same when, in 1956, he briefly took a job with Archibald Quincy Jones at just the time that Jones and Emmons were building a steel house in San Mateo, California, for the innovative property developer Joseph Eichler. Both Eichler and John Entenza, the editor of *Arts & Architecture*, were actively promoting good modern design for the ordinary house and were equally drawn to the possibilities offered by lightweight steel house construction; indeed, Soriano had built a steel house for Eichler just the previous year in Palo Alto, California. By now the vocabulary of glazed walls, profiled steel roof and exposed steel frame was the basis of Koenig's palette; it was only time before he found the right client so that Entenza could invite him into the Program. When he did, this turned out to be a psychologist, Walter Bailey, and his wife Mary. The Baileys had no children and so here was an opportunity for Koenig to develop an open-plan design which took maximum benefit of the wide spans which the steel frame could provide.

The house itself was framed up with four double-span steel bents—prefabricated rectangular frames—44 feet wide and 9 feet high. A further three bents, of half the width, framed the entranceway and carport. The steel dimensions were the same as both Soriano and Jones had used in their Eichler houses, 4-inch H-section columns and 8-inch I-section beams, but whereas Soriano had cantilevered his beams out from

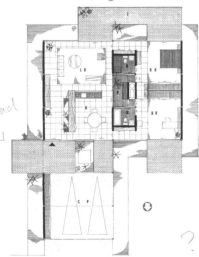

the side of the house, Koenig, like Jones, tucked his in under the eaves. To accommodate standard-size sheets of profiled-metal roofing deck, Jones had placed h bents at 8-foot centres but Koenig, like Soriano, chose, for greater economy, the wid spacing of 10 feet. To this arrangement Koenig added a small, open-air fountain cou in the centrally-placed bathroom core which separated the living spaces from t sleeping spaces. This court opened onto the kitchen and allowed light and fresh a into the centre of the house.

The house was arranged on a north-south axis, the carport and entranceway to t north leading through to the fully-glazed south wall where the best view was obtaine To the west was a scrubby hillside and to the east, the road. Consequently the side wa were clad with interlocking steel panels, painted white, like the underside of the ro deck, in contrast to the black lines of the frame. Set around the house was a shallo reflecting pool bridged over, on the north and south elevations, by low platforms pav in red brick and framed in steel. Here the Bellevue sliding glass doors could withdrawn to allow the interior to spread out into the landscape. And from the eave gentle jets of water would spill into the pools, bending the rectilinear reflection as if

Opposite page, above:
View from the dining area back towards the carport

Opposite page, below:
The plan, showing how the house is surrounded by reflecting pools and brick patios 露台

The entranceway separates the carport from the house.

Perspective drawing of south front

View from the entranceway through to the living area, showing the reflecting pool fed by water spouts.

Perspective drawing of internal court

mock the purity of the form. When interviewed, Koenig recalled how John Entenza described the house: "a very pristine, clean design. Two details, one north-south, one east-west. One material for the roof, same one for the walls. Minimal house, maximum space."

For many architects and critics, the Bailey House is not just the high point of the Case Study House Program but also Koenig's best building. At the time it was recognised with a 1959 Sunset Magazine Honor Award, and the following year with an Award of Merit presented by the AIA in cooperation with *House and Home* and *Life* magazine. This was the AIA Homes for Better Living Award and it was presented at the AIA 1960 Convention held on 21 April that year at the Mark Hopkins Hotel in San Francisco. Koenig went up to San Francisco to accept the award and the ceremony is marked off in his programme. In 2001 the AIA made a further award, the AIA California Council 25 Year Award, "for excellence in design of Case Study House #21 (Bailey House)." The Bailey House represents the ultimate refinement of an ideal developed by Koenig in his early houses and built upon through his experience with Soriano and Quincy Jones. It

Pierre Koenig often posed with models to people his own buildings for publicity photographs.

Below:
The internal court with the bathroom beyond

was the simplest of solutions achieved in, apparently, the most effortless way and was a remarkable achievement for such a young man.

So it is perhaps surprising that by the time Dan Cracchiolo, a film producer at Warner Brothers, bought the house almost forty years later, it had suffered considerably. So he asked Koenig to restore it. "Even though I knew what had been going on in this house," Koenig told David Hay, "it was a great shock to see it. My houses are like children to me."

The restoration took Koenig longer to complete than it had taken him to build the house and the exactitude of the work was recognised by both the City of Los Angeles and the Los Angeles Conservancy. On behalf of the City, the Mayor, Richard Riordan, and the Los Angeles Cultural Heritage Commission awarded Koenig the Historic Preservation 2000 Award of Excellence for "the outstanding rehabilitation of Bailey House". Likewise, the Los Angeles Conservancy gave him their Preservation Award 2000, "For the exemplary renovation, spearheaded by the original architect, of one of Los Angeles' original Case Study Houses, restoring a deteriorated and neglected steel

and glass home to its rightful place as a visual symbol of Los Angeles Modern residential architecture."

But Cracchiolo soon sold the house, the new owner, Michael LaFetra also being from the movie industry. Speaking later of Koenig's commitment, LaFetra told Eryn Brown at the *Los Angeles Times* that, within a week of buying the house, he received a message on his telephone answering machine: "Hello, this is Pierre, your architect, and I want to talk." What Koenig wanted to say was simple, to the point and reflected his sense of ownership. He told LaFetra that he ought not to have to change anything in the house but, if he needed to, he should get in touch with him.

The living area, where glass sliders open directly on to the patio

Left:
The master bedroom opens directly on to the patio.

patio 设计的原点

1960 · Seidel House

2727 Mandeville Canyon Road, Los Angeles, California
▸ Extended as Rollé House, 1984, 1994

Koenig's attitude towards his buildings was protective. They were, as he had said, his children. So it is not surprising that when the Seidel House was extended in 1984 and again in 1994, it was to Koenig that the new owners turned. The house was built as a speculation by Tom Seidel, a building contractor, and Jean Hagan and it was Seidel who again took on the job when the house was first extended twenty-four years later.

The site was not promising: a long, narrow shelf with unstable soil conditions cut out of the steep gradient on the west side of Mandeville Canyon. To accommodate this, Koenig reduced the structure to a minimum number of point loads supported on concrete caissons sunk 15 feet into the ground. The result was a steel frame comprising six bents, each spanning 24 feet and made up of 4-inch H-section columns and 10-inch I-section beams. These were placed irregularly at 32-foot and 16-foot centres, thus defining the larger living and sleeping zones and the smaller, internal courtyards or patios which separated them. An end bay of 20 feet accommodated the carport. The longer than usual 32-foot span was achieved by using 16-gauge T-section steel roofing deck with a 6-inch web.

The living area, with its brick fireplace and glazed side wall

The linear nature of the plan and the manner in which the different zones were separated by courtyard spaces was not unlike the plan adopted by Charles and Ray Eames in their Case Study House #8, built on a similarly narrow site in Pacific Palisades in 1949. Here, as in Koenig's solution, the carport was at one end and the living room and sheltered sun deck were at the other, while an external walkway ran the length of the house linking the disparate spaces. But there the similarities end for

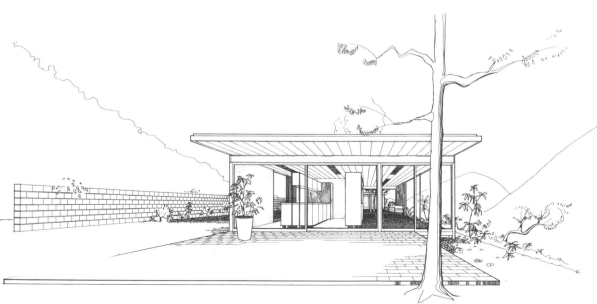

**The carport is set within the structural frame
of the house.**

whereas the Eames House is noticeable for its fragility and colourful transparency,
Koenig's design was robust and uncompromising. The 5-foot overhang at the south
end and the deep sections of the I-beams and the roof deck emphasised the horizontal
while the vertically-placed 20-gauge double-rib steel decking used for the exterior walls
provided a sense of enclosure quite lacking at the Eames House.

Compared with the Bailey House, however, the plan was not so rigorous. Although
a cross-axial entrance separated effectively the living and sleeping zones, the linearity
of the plan was compromised by large side windows looking down from the family area
towards the road. Blind side walls in this position might well have resulted, owing to
the sheltered nature of the site, in a cold and gloomy interior, but the introduction of
a 20-foot glazed side wall appears to imbalance the composition. Nevertheless, it
provides a sense of drama and openness suggestive of Case Study House #22 and the
house was given an AIA Sunset Magazine Award for 1961–1962.

In extending the house for Della and Gary Rollé in 1984, Koenig designed a new
bedroom, bathroom and den unit which sat above the existing living zone, its independent structure straddling but not touching the older building. The same approach
was used for the second addition, another set of rooms comprising an all-purpose
room, a work area and more bathrooms, being hung above the old sleeping zone. This

The second addition in 1994 extended the
upper storey across the original bed and
bathrooms.

Right:
Plan of the house before the additions

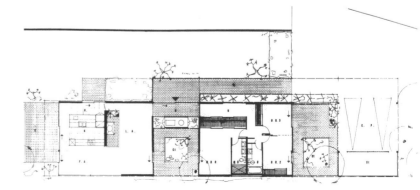

The new atrium, created following the
extension of the upper storey in 1994

allowed Koenig to glaze in, to full height, the courtyard which had separated the two
zones, thus creating a 25-foot atrium which rose up to a clerestory and was not unlike
the central space which he was to create in his own house in Brentwood the following
year. In recasting the Seidel House as the Rollé House, Koenig hid the more con-
structivist qualities of the H-columns and I-beams, introducing cleaner box sections
and reducing the pale blue and avocado paintwork of the old building to shades of grey.

The first addition in 1984 placed a new storey on top of the living areas.

Right:
The kitchen and dining area

Opposite page:
Exposed steelworks help define the interior spaces while the exposed roofing deck unites them.

1960 ▸ Stahl House

Case Study House #22
1636 Woods Drive, Los Angeles, California

opposite page:
he living and dining area, with an oblique
ew of the Hollywood hills beyond

the house and carport from the road

the plan, showing the swimming pool, patios
nd linking platforms

The deep beams and broad-spanning roofing deck which facilitated the minimal structure at the Seidel House characterised the new house which Koenig build for Carlotta and C. H. 'Buck' Stahl in 1960. Adopted by John Entenza as Case Study House #22, it became the most famous house of the programme and was even rebuilt at the Museum of Contemporary Art's Temporary Contemporary building in Los Angeles as part of the 1989 exhibit 'Blueprints for Modern Living, History and Legacy of the Case Study House Program'. Thus it was the only Case Study House to be built twice.

Koenig described the position of the house, high above Sunset Boulevard, as being "on an eagle's nest site in the Hollywood hills". Carlotta and Buck Stahl had seen the plot one weekend while staying in an apartment on an opposite hillside. The owner just happened to be there and the purchase was completed in two and a half hours. Buck Stahl, as Koenig recalled, he had some idea of how he wanted the house to be: "The owner wanted a clear and unobstructed view of 270 degrees and this is the only way we could do it, the way I did it. It's all glass," he explained, "all the way around, except for the front which is solid ... Then the back side is all glass for 270 degrees. It has got a magnificent view. It's a neutral statement. The view is important. The house is supposed to fit in with the environment and relate to it. You don't see the house when you're in it, you see the view and you're living with the environment, the outside ... That's how Case Study House #22 was designed and why it was designed."

Opposite page, above:
Steel beams support the roof deck and probe the space beyond.

Opposite page, below:
The perspective drawing emphasises the explosive nature of the design.

The concrete T-beam slab was supported on 35-foot caissons sunk into the hillside.

Case Study House #22 differed from its predecessor in that it was concerned less with the possibilities of prefabrication and the use of standardised components than it was with the potential of the materials. Whereas the steel bents in the earlier Case Study House had been set on 10-foot centres, here a 20-foot square grid was adopted, thus doubling the span, but not extending it as far as at the Seidel House. 12-inch I-section beams, as at the Seidel House, were used but this time a shallower roof deck of 5 inches was specified. The familiar 4-inch H-section columns were employed again.

Whereas both Case Study House #21 and the Seidel House were contained, the steel frames forming closed rectangles, here at the new Case Study House the beams were allowed to extend far beyond their columns, supporting the long cantilevers of the roof deck and giving the cliff-top building every appearance of a bird about to lift off in flight. Thus the eagle metaphor was retained.

The sense of outreach which the building expressed was no illusion. As Koenig explained, "On the land, the good land, we put a pool and carport; and the house, in a sense, is off on the space ... The house is on piers and cantilevers, and with big overhangs. A little different approach for me." Thus the frame was supported on 35-foot concrete caissons sunk into the hillside while the cantilevered concrete floor was upheld by 30-inch deep reinforced concrete beams. The house was arranged on an L-shaped plan, the sleeping accommodation along one arm and the living, extending into space, along the other. Where they met were the bathrooms.

As if to emphasise the transience of the site, Koenig placed the swimming pool within the angle of the building, allowing the water to almost lap the bedroom windows and thus interrupt the entrance route from the carport. The result is that the land appears to dematerialise, the pool providing reflections of the overhanging eaves and of the sky, while the narrow strip of paving around the pool, and the platforms which bridge the water outside the bedrooms, offer no great sense of stability or of enclosure.

The transparency which the glazed walls provided was emphasised by the openness of the plan and the overhanging roof deck which appeared to run uninterrupted

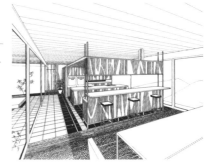

Perspective drawing of the kitchen and breakfast bar

Above:
The kitchen was defined by its suspended ceiling and "floating" counters.

The living area with the lights of Los Angeles beyond

rom side to side. Externally, the only solid wall was the one which separated the bed-
ooms from the road and the carport. It was clad vertically with roof decking. Internally,
vith the exception of the enclosed dressing room, there was just one dividing wall and
hat was between the two bedrooms. From any point in the house, the view was to the
distant horizon and the few fittings which were necessary were carefully arranged so as
not to disrupt the sightlines. The focus of the living area, clearly visible from outside,
vas a rectangular chimney breast or canopy which appeared to hang from the ceiling;
similarly, the kitchen was a space within a space, its volume defined by an independent suspended ceiling and the centre- and end-counters which seemed to float above
the continuous floor plane. As Koenig explained, he never designed the house for
people to look at. "All my statements are not inward — look at the house, look at the
form of it, look at the shape. I don't do that. I look outward and the people inside are
projected outward to whatever is around them. That's my attitude towards the
building."

Since 1962, the use of the house as a set for movies and advertisements has provided the Stahls with a second income. If Carlotta now needs to vacate the house

47

The bedrooms back onto the street wall and open onto the swimming pool.

Opposite page, above:
The transparency of the house allows oblique views from one space to another and through to the city beyond.

斜的 阻挡的

Opposite page, below:
A view which is never seen: a perspective drawing of the house taken from high above the roof of the Château Marmont

during a shoot, she takes a room at the Château Marmont, just below the house, or Sunset Boulevard. Here she asks for a room without a view. One can have too much of a good thing.

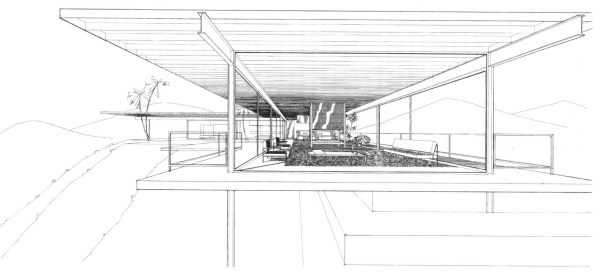

1962 ▸ Johnson House

54 La Rancheria, Carmel Valley, California
▸ Extended as Riebe House, 1995

xterior from south-west following the
dditions of 1995

Despite the considerable publicity which *Arts & Architecture* gave to his architecture, Koenig rarely received commissions from northern California. But Cyrus and Elizabeth Johnson had seen his houses in the magazine and determined to build one for themselves in northern California. Carmel Valley is in the hot hinterland, some ten miles from Carmel and the Pacific Ocean. Climatically, it was not unlike southern California, but it was an area where Spanish styles of architecture predominated.

The site which the Johnsons had bought on La Rancheria faced south, was planted with live oaks, and sloped away from the road with views of distant rolling hills beyond. It was, in a sense, not unlike the site for the Case Study House #22, and Koenig treated it similarly. Instead of building a swimming pool, he levelled and strengthened the site by constructing an in-situ concrete single-storey structure which pushed out into the landscape and, once encased in back-fill, effectively became a basement. Then on top of this, at road level, he arranged the carport, entrance and sleeping accommodation along the northern edge and the kitchen and living room in a glazed, projecting wing to the south. Thus the L-shaped plan of the living accommodation was a mirror image of Case Study House #22. The only change was that he moved the entrance and carport to the other end of the bedroom wing, which gave the structure a T-shaped, rather than L-shaped, footprint.

In the Case Study House, the carport had formed the entrance to the property rather than the building itself: that was accessed across the bridges along the side of the swimming pool. Here, at the Johnson House, a small workshop separated the bedroom wing from the carport and in so doing created a covered entranceway with a framed view along the west side of the living-room wing. Off this, at the point of juncture of the living and sleeping accommodation, was the entrance hall. Whereas at the Case Study House, the house was entered on the inside corner of the L-shaped plan, at the Johnson House it was entered on the outside. Yet in both cases, the position of the free-standing kitchen directed the visitor towards the living room and central fireplace beyond.

As in the Case Study House, Koenig adopted a 20-foot-square grid with deep steel beams running the length of the living room wing and projecting into space beyond. Whereas at the Case Study House the beam ends had been cut off square, here they were tapered to reflect more accurately the loading of the cantilever, and also to give the elevation a sense of sleek refinement. A 6-inch T-section roofing deck, deeper than at the Case Study House, spanned the beams and extended to provide a 7-foot overhang all around. As well as sheltering the interior from solar gain, the overhanging roof provided, as Koenig wrote in the house description, "a feeling of indoor-outdoor living." Once more, Koenig used 8x10-foot glass sliders to enclose the living room wing and the south-facing façade of the bedrooms, but he introduced, at the Johnsons' request, a 20-foot solid wall panel on the west side of the living room to provide shelter for furniture and a piano. This he finished internally with natural teak panelling. Externally, the house was clad with vertically-hung decking painted a warm beige, which picked up

View along the side of the living area towards
the new guest bedrooms

Floor plan showing additions of 1995

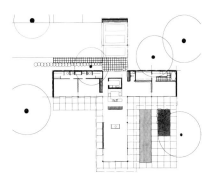

漂白

the bleached oak of the flooring within. The ceilings, as was now standard in his build
ings, consisted of the exposed roofing deck, painted white.

In this house, as in the Case Study House, the choice of a 20-foot-square grid di
not fully exploit the structural potential of the steelwork, even though the projectin
roof beams under the cantilever at the southern end suggest a linear form. It was, how
ever, a necessary choice since the bi-directional nature of the L- and T-shaped gri
would not allow one direction to be dominant. At the contemporaneous Oberma
House, as will be shown, the linear nature of the plan allowed Koenig to run his fram
mono-directionally and then to brace it with structural roof decking.

In 1995 Koenig returned to Carmel Valley to restore and extend the house for Fred an
Cynthia Riebe. Now it was less of a curiosity, other modern houses having been bui
nearby. The restoration involved upgrading the kitchen, which was extended back into th
bedroom wing to allow space for a breakfast bar. The worktop and suspended cabinet
which had screened the kitchen from the living room were now redesigned as a storag
wall and taken up to the underside of the roofing deck, while a new suspended ceilin
with a rooflight, was inserted behind to define the space and help provide a greater sens
of enclosure. More drastic was the rearranging and extension of the bedroom wing itsel
First of all, the carport and workshop were replaced by two guest bedrooms, which coul
be achieved easily enough under the existing roofing deck. A new carport was the
built at right-angles to the old and in line with the living-room wing. This converted th

The new entranceway and carport added in 1995

The kitchen and breakfast bar following the remodelling of the house.

The living area remained largely unaltered in the remodelling of 1995

T-shaped plan into a cruciform plan. The entrance now was on the north side of the bedroom wing and a new entranceway was created where the old master bathroom and dressing room had been. They were now located, together with the new master bedroom, at the far east end of the bedroom wing, with a den positioned between this and the kitchen. Thus the building could become more of a family house.

In his written description of the house, Koenig quoted the Johnsons as saying that their house would be "a permanent home with an ageless design—a house that will still be here for our grandchildren". Although it never became their grandchildren's house, the ease with which Koenig adapted the house for the Riebes demonstrated the flexibility of the system and how it could serve couples and larger family units equally well. In concluding his description he wrote, "The Johnsons feel their steel-framed home will set the pattern for [the] construction of homes in the future. The structure will need minimum maintenance, as permanent materials are used which will not crack or rot and are not affected by vermin or fungus." Although the advantages were clear, the marketability of these houses was still very limited and the clients who came to Koenig for them were very specific in their brief and their choice of site.

wo guest bedrooms and a patio replaced the
arage and workshop in 1995.

loor plan of original design

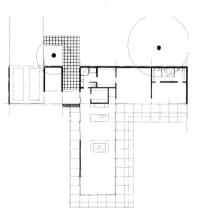

1962·Oberman House

5200 Crestwind Drive, Palos Verdes, California

In the same way that the landscape and swimming pool at Case Study House #22 were a function of the building, at the Oberman House in Palos Verdes the house and pool have an interdependent relationship. The client's request was for an unlimited view and the complete integration of the pool with everyday life. The result was a fully glazed 69-foot-long rigid steel-framed building with the 60-foot pool running parallel, its L-shaped plan responding to the trapezoidal nature of the site.

Palos Verdes is a hilly peninsula of now expensive residential property pushing out into the Pacific Ocean and separating Long Beach and San Pedro Bay from the popular beach communities to the north. The site which Mayor Oberman offered Koenig had extensive views of the ocean to the south and west, and Koenig made the best use of this by centralising the ancillary functions as a core within the plan and wrapping the peripheral living spaces in glass. Once again, the clients' aspirations were not matched by their budget, and Koenig had to design with economy while the Obermans acted as their own building contractors.

In his earliest buildings, such as the Koenig House #1 and the Lamel House, Koenig had used steel beams to span the length of the building, thus achieving maximum efficiency with the structure. But from the Low-Cost Production House (built as the Burwash House in Tujunga, 1957) onwards, he had either placed the beams across the shorter span or, as in Case Study House #22 and the Johnson House, used a square grid. Now at the Oberman House Koenig chose once again to span the longer distance with the primary structure but, to span the shorter distance, he used a structural roofing deck in place of beams. The result was innovatory. The primary structure ran the length of the house, north/south, and comprised 4-inch H-section columns set at 23-foot centres connected by 12-inch I-section steel beams. Arranged in four parallel but not equidistant rows, these frames allowed Koenig to place his entrance axis and kitchen/bathroom core off centre, thus giving more space for the rooms that faced the pool. The secondary, east/west structure was achieved with 4-inch T-section structural roofing deck except where 4-inch beams spanned the patio. The use of such a roofing deck enabled him to avoid having to take his major structural members, which should be of the same depth, across intermediate spans of differing widths. The result was a consistently deep frieze running the length of the pool-side elevation and providing visual strength and unity, as well as a variety of spaces within which were not compromised by the demands of symmetrical planning.

The long elevation to the pool was divided into four bays, two for the house, one for the patio and the last, separated by a steel and wire boundary fence, for the carport and entranceway. At the rear of this were positioned, for acoustic separation, the utility rooms. The four upstanding I-section beams which spanned the patio broke the constant line of the eaves and thus defined the space below, which itself was subdivided by a shallow steel roofing deck which marked the axial entrance route. This terminated in the walnut fascia of the kitchen as at Case Study House #22, a space within a space, to one side of which was the dining room and to the other, the breakfast room. Each, in

The view on approaching the house

Right:
Plan, showing the axial entranceway and
clearly defined outdoor and indoor zones

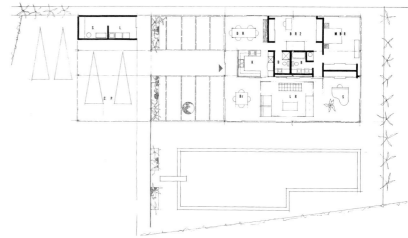

Glass sliders withdraw to allow the house and poolside patio to become one space.

turn, opened back onto their own part of the patio. Behind the kitchen/bathroom core, and to the left was the sleeping accommodation, and to the right, along the poolside façade, were the living area and the study with its grand piano, for the Obermans were musicians.

The exposed nature of the site, with its views to Santa Catalina Island beyond, meant that it was very windy and consequently Koenig had to design the house without the benefit of shady overhangs, which would have been subject to uplift, or of sheltering trees, which would never have got established. So Koolshade louvred screens slide along the south and west walls to reduce the solar gain, and the patios and fire-pit are tucked in behind the bulk of the house and out of the wind.

Koenig extended the purity of the white-painted steel frame into the interior, where the floor was white terrazzo and the ceilings were panels of white acoustic board or obscured glass (with fluorescent lights behind) set between the ribs of the roofing deck. Although the kitchen units stopped short of the ceiling, allowing the space to flow on through, the long storage wall which made up the east side of the living room extended from floor to ceiling and, with the full-height white curtains which ran the

The living area with the dining area beyond

length of the glazed walls, provided the room with an unexpected sense of enclosure. Perhaps this was a further response to the winds.

In 1967, the City of Los Angeles and the AIA Southern California Chapter sponsored an 'Architectural Grand Prix of the Greater Los Angeles Area on the 186th Birthday of the City of Los Angeles.' Under the Presidency of another Case Study House architect, Edward Killingsworth, the AIA SC Chapter selected the 36 most significant buildings erected in Los Angeles since 1947. The one Koenig design included was the Oberman House. The citation said: "A fine example of industrial materials imaginatively employed for a well-organized, well-detailed residence. Indoor-outdoor functions are directly related and the over-all [sic] result suggests a richness of living possibilities." It was an accolade a little overdue, for the American Iron and Steel Institute had already cited the Oberman House 'for Excellence for Use of Structural Steel' in 1963. Koenig was, as the *Los Angeles Times* reported on 28 April that year, the only architect in Southern California to receive this award, although California architects, designers and engineers received half of the awards made. Indeed, the Chairman of Senate at the University of Southern California had written to him at the School of Architecture

1. Introduction.   Analysis.   2个 house.

400字 ← 17 part.

共 4 part.

—怎么来写17段公注无格
段落不要好序排一17.

Job List.
14 × 50.
700.
600.

Design strategy?

可以试着写17段段落

400   身份 & 身份.

(400个 17段开始.

有7, 4/17 3次

Stahl House.

→ Bailey house   中庭

Structure

记23 (记得记).

structure.
construction technique.

California design. Pab.

600 — 400 — 150.
— 300 —

Structure 2"

construction tech seq.

A B C D E F G H I J K L M N O P Q R S T U V W X Y Z

家养·小金鱼.
低头.
对. 在这行船.
鱼鳞2(鱼鳞)3.

mahila life Park
Colophonir

在乡下，此处好看，有走近就变看热闹。

structure — Frame Plan.

aims to why

Koenig

1200. g.oo
1800   ΣAM

FOOTING Section.

Outdoor and indoor spaces merge beneath the continuous roof deck to create a unified whole.

saying, "Your recognition in this way reflects not only on your own position but also the stature of the University as a whole."

It would seem, however, that the Obermans did not stay long to enjoy either their house or its recognition. In November 1968, the realtors Caldwell, Banker and Company wrote to Koenig to tell him that they had been instructed to place the house on the market with an asking price of $118,500. Twelve years later it was on the market again but the price was now $220,000.

1963 ▸ Iwata House

912 Summit Place, Monterey Park, California

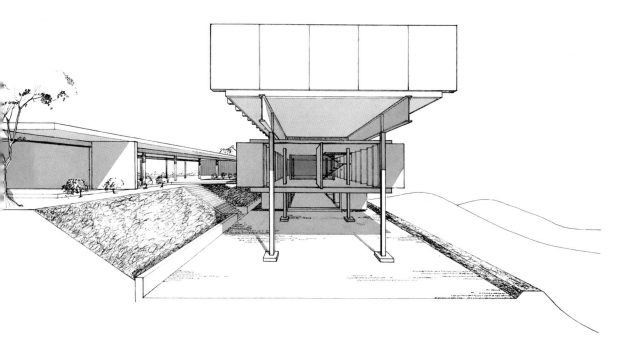

The perspective drawing emphasises the structural concept behind the design.

The axial entranceway separates the carport from the swimming pool.

The house which Koenig built for Richard and Vicki Iwata and their five children suggests, at first appearance, a major departure from the transparent steel box which, by 1963, had become almost a trade mark. But what it actually shows is that Koenig was not bound to such limitations and that every design was adjusted to meet the client's requirements. Now here were clients with very different demands and so a noticeably different solution emerged.

The site in Monterey Park, an inland community on the edge of the San Gabriel Mountains, was wedge-shaped, narrowest by the access road and broadest at the far end where the land fell away steeply. Koenig's options, therefore, were either to build a long, thin house on the narrow, flat land nearest the road, or to take up the width of the site and perch his building on the slope. It was the latter which he chose, for to build on a slope allowed him to design in cross-section as well as in plan.

The entry to the house was processional, a long straight pathway which flanked the pool and passed through the entry pavilion, which contained the changing rooms and the carport, before crossing a slender bridge into the house, where it terminated at the central point of the stairs. Here the living spaces spread out to either side, the dining room, kitchen and family room to the left and the living room to the right, with the music room and den beyond. This whole area, excluding the balconies at either end, measured about 70x20 feet, proportions which leave the space seeming pinched and in need of the fully glazed walls which are denied. Instead, fins are added to the long external wall which, while controlling solar gain, obscure cross-views of the landscape beyond.

A perspective drawing of an earlier version of
the scheme, with the swimming pool and
carport removed and the upper storey one bay
longer

From this central level, the stairs went up to the bedroom floor, where there was also a
library, study, sewing room and radio room, and down to the children's play floor which
included a workshop. A sense of hierarchy ran through the levels, from the most flex
ible spaces at the bottom to the most cellular at the top. This was reflected across the
rear elevation in the repetition of fins at each level, the greatest number at the top and
the least at the bottom. Thus while the specific function of each level, and of certain
elements, could be recognised from the outside, the relative need for privacy was
retained. This was most noticeable, for example, at the top level, where the multitude
of fins made it difficult to distinguish one bedroom from the next, although the blank
panels in two of the bays do suggest a different function. Other features, such as the
stair shaft, stand out clearly, as does the protruding bay to one side, but only a know
ledge of the plan would allow this to be identified as the pantry.

The various contemporary descriptions of the building refer to 'a tree-like, canti
levered steel frame with a secondary wood system integrated". This, no doubt, was
Koenig's terminology in a way, but it was not a helpful description, for this tree would
have six trunks. The steel frame, in fact, was arranged in the same way as that at the
Oberman House, the principal structural beams running in parallel for the length
rather than the width, of the house. Set about 14 feet from the other, each beam was
supported by three 8x8-inch square section columns at 35-foot centres. The top floor
which demanded the largest cantilever, was supported on 27-inch deep I-sections; the
middle floor on 21-inch I-sections. The lowest floor sat on the ground. A secondary
structure of 16-inch I-sections, spanning the long beams and expressed externally, fur
ther supported the top floor, thus adding to the sense of compartmentalisation which
the layered design suggested. In reality, the separation between the floors provided a
crawl space for electrical and mechanical services and enhanced acoustic separation.

The flexibility of the lower floors was in stark contrast to the cellular arrangement of
the top floor, where the rear elevation was divided into nine equal bays, six for bed
rooms and the other three for the library, the radio room and a patio which merged

64

Fins combat solar gain as well as suggesting the relative privacy of the spaces within.

Below:
Floor plans (top to bottom): bedroom level, family level with entrance bridges, basement level with playroom and workshop, carport and pool-house

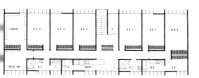

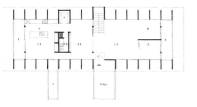

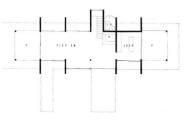

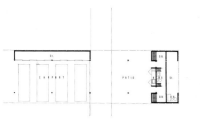

with the stair shaft. Only the library and the master bedroom extended the full depth of the floor plate, each accommodating, in an almost symmetrical manner, storage for books and clothes respectively. A spine corridor, set off-centre, linked them. All the other rooms, which were essentially identical, had a shallower plan and opened off one side of the corridor, on the other side of which were three bathrooms, the study and the sewing room. It was a tight, almost institutional plan but, within the confines of a framed structure, must have worked.

The defining feature of the building is the fins. Their function, as has been suggested, was to combat solar gain. With the rear of the building facing south-east, their positioning would have welcomed morning sun but the more the sun moved to the south, the more the fins would have excluded it. Thus the use of fins on the north-east entrance elevation is questionable, but they would nevertheless have excluded summer sun late in the day, by which time the building would require no more heating. The location of the fins was determined by tests of a model on a heliodon, where the position of the sun at any time on any day of the year could be simulated and the shadows measured. Koenig therefore placed the fins close together on the bedroom level, where the rooms were narrow, while on the lower levels, where the rooms were larger, the fins were positioned further apart. Thus the permitted solar gain was in proportion to the spaces which it heated.

The house, nevertheless, was fitted ready for the installation of air-conditioning. It might have been of this house that Christopher Reed, writing Koenig's obituary, described how at one client's request, Koenig had installed the ducts, though not the machines, for air-conditioning. He had asked the client to depend upon natural ventilation for just one year but, "In less than a year," he is quoted as saying, "the client phoned to say he didn't need air-conditioning."

1963 · Beagles House

17446 Revello Drive, Los Angeles, California

Opposite page:
The open circulation core, punctured by the tall flue of the log stove, unites the levels.

Right:
The entranceway and the children's small enclosed patio face onto the street.

Below:
Perched on the hillside, the house looks out towards the Pacific Ocean.

Lower floor plan
The dining and children's areas are on the floor above.

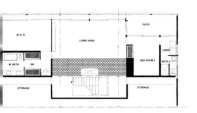

The house which Koenig built for Bob and Alice Beagles was, like the Iwata House, mono-directional. From the street it was almost unnoticeable, a low, glazed elevation which suggested a pavilion but at the rear, where the ground fell steeply away, the house developed into two broad, balconied floors suspended high above the escarpment. Here the view swept across the Palisades and down to the Pacific.

Whereas Koenig had used a sloping site before, as at the Stahl House and Iwata House, he had hung the building on the edge, at the Beagles House he now encouraged it to step out over the void. The two-storey arrangement demanded access at the upper level so Koenig adopted what he called 'an inverted plan', placing the kitchen, dining room, playroom and two bedrooms at street level, with the living room and master bedroom and guest room on the floor below. Only the playroom addressed the street, but even this was secluded by a small, enclosed patio; all the other rooms took in the view.

Although the split-use arrangement reflected the differing requirements of the parents and their two small daughters, there was no sense of separation internally. An open circulation core, punctured by the tall flue of the log stove, rose through the centre of the plan, linking both floors and allowing oblique views from the living room below to the playroom above.

While the street elevation appears tightly glazed—even the garage doors are glass sliders—the ocean-side of the house suggests layers of space. Outermost is the frame

The living area with its patio beyond

Below:
Perspective drawing of the street elevation
suggesting that the house is a small, tightly
contained pavilion

and the balcony railings, behind which the full-height glazing is set back, first some 18 inches and then 8 feet and 12 feet to provide open patio areas. The resulting ambiguity, in contrast to the stuccoed side walls, leaves this building edge undefined and the landscape apparently within easy reach.

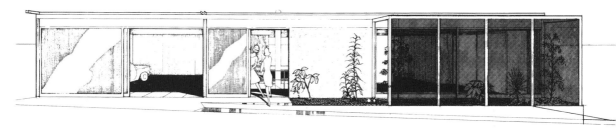

The breakfast bar with its patio beyond

Below:
The dining area on the upper level

1971–1976 ▸ Chemehuevi Prefabricated Housing Tract

Havasu Lake, California

A low-cost tribal house for the desert environment

Construction work in the desert

One intention of the Case Study House Program had been to provide affordable houses for ordinary Americans, and for Koenig this meant prefabrication and factory production. "My desire," he later told Alison Arieff and Bryan Burkhart, "was to make affordable houses for as many people as possible. I live for the day to see these houses popping out of a production line, and what a joy that would be!" His initial demonstration of this had been in the Burwash House in Tujunga, California, published in *Arts & Architecture* in March 1957 as a low-cost production house: "To combat today's high cost of building and to produce a competitive house with features not ordinarily found in mass-produced houses, every up-to-date building method will be used." Despite its promise, the low-cost production house remained a one-off. However, in January 1961 *Arts & Architecture* showed his scheme for six factory-made houses which had been manufactured in Detroit, the home of the motor industry, and shipped up to Canada to a site at St Jean, Quebec. Built with a steel frame and clad with insulated metal sandwich panels developed by the R.C. Mahon Company and capable of withstanding indoor/outdoor temperature difference of 160°F, these houses offered a solution to building in an extreme climate. "It is a definite advantage," Koenig wrote, "to be able to prefabricate houses in a plant during the winter period so that more may be constructed during the short summer. It is also advantageous to be able to erect the entire shell with the roofing immediately so that all other work can be done under cover, thus extending the working year. This also affects the economy of the community where the work year is short."

Whereas Quebec could be very cold, the Senoran desert, located along the California/Arizona border from Needles in the north to Yuma in the south, could be

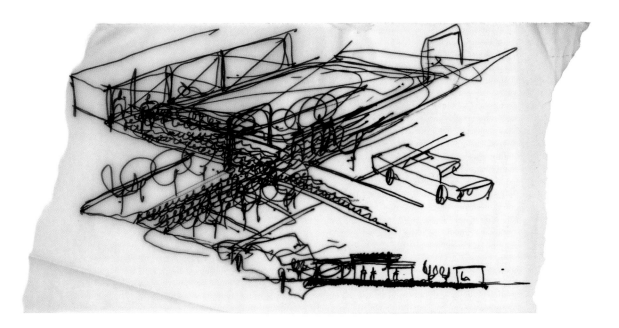

extremely hot. Parts of the desert share with Death Valley the highest and most sustained air temperatures in North America; temperatures of 90°F or more may occur in February and periods of up to three months with temperatures rising to 100°F are not exceptional. It was in such a climate, 40 miles south of Needles, along the Colorado River on the California side of Lake Havasu, where the Chemehuevi Indian Reservation was found. Over the years, the Chemehuevi tribe had become scattered, but in 1968 they had successfully begun to reorganise and by the end of 1970 were legally established as a tribe, with a tribal council and a chairman, Ralph Esquerra.

In 1971 the Dependency Prevention Commission of San Bernardino County asked the University of Southern California to make preliminary investigations for a development plan for the Reservation, because the Chemehuevi tribe, while recognising their desperate need for economic independence, wished at the same time not to despoil their heartland. This plan was to comprise an exploratory land-use study of the Reservation, the establishing of alternative planning strategies for tribal housing development, and the design of low-cost tribal houses for the desert environment. The Chemehuevi Project, as it became known, was undertaken over ten weeks by 21 third-year undergraduates from the School of Architecture, led by three professors, Keith Grey, Peter Rodemeier and Pierre Koenig. The third phase of the project, the design of low-cost tribal housing, was directed by Koenig.

Koenig's team recognised the need for a housing type which would attract people of the same background but who, because of the dispersal of the tribe, had developed different life-styles. The choice of an industrialised structure brought with it all the

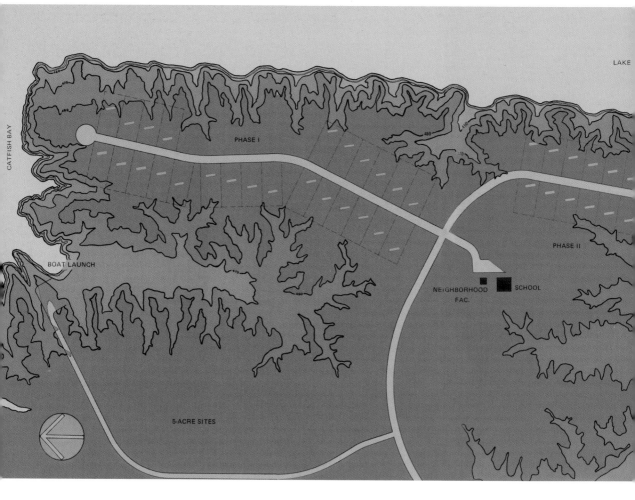

Site plan, showing the remote nature of the community

benefits of quick erection in an unfriendly climate, as well as the possibility of modula variation to meet specific requirements. Six basic steel-framed house types wer developed specifically in response to the desert conditions and input from members c the tribe. The houses ranged from a 400-square-foot one-bedroom and front porch c carport model to a 1200-square-foot model with four bedrooms, an interior patio an two carports. The buildings were to be orientated with their backs to the north win and designed with full-length glazing to provide views of the southern horizon from seated position of the floor. Insulated cladding panels, as used in the Canadian projec kept the buildings cool while shaded front porches and carports and, in the large models, internal courtyards, allowed for air circulation. Due to the modular construc tion, a wide variety of plan forms were available based on a 40-inch grid. This was s versatile, that it was extended to the design of the public facilities including the schoo recreation centre, medical building and stables.

The basic structure was a series of 20-foot steel bents positioned at 10 feet centre and fixed to concrete footings. The 40-inch wide cladding panels provided structura rigidity, one length being used for the walls and another, in a single 10-foot length, fo the roof. 10-foot overhangs protected the glazed south front from the high midday sur

The modular, component-based design allows for degrees of variation within the same basic form.

while the east and west side walls were kept largely free of windows to prevent solar gain from the morning or evening sun. The interior was lined with 4-inch timber studwork to provide clearance for the insulation and to minimise heat transfer, and finished with gypsum plaster-board. Bathroom and kitchen units were to be pre-fabricated and brought to site ready for installation.

The University of Southern California published its plan for the Chemehuevi Project in July 1971. Well-received and reported in the press, it encouraged the Office of Economic Opportunity to award the Dependency Prevention Commission a further $ 90,000, which allowed the project to continue for three more years. Once all funding was exhausted, Koenig took the work on himself for another two years. Although he lobbied state and federal agencies extensively, the project, he later told James Steele and David Jenkins, was defeated by political inertia. "The houses we had proposed were too nice. The politicians didn't want the Chemehuevi to have better houses than they had themselves, so they did nothing."

1979 ▸ Burton Pole-House

31371 Pacific Coast Highway, Malibu, California

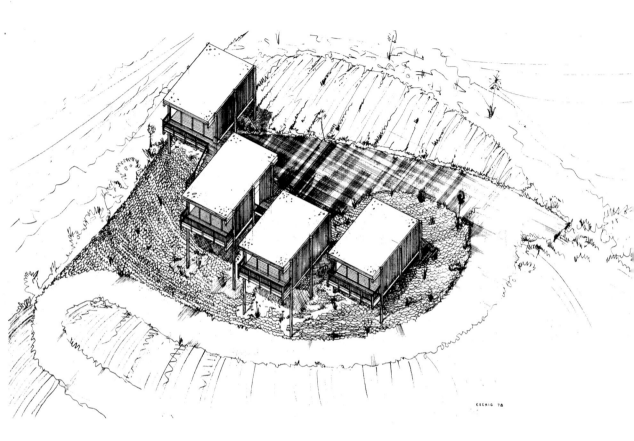

Aerial perspective drawing showing the completed design

The multiple-unit modular planning lessons of the Chemehuevi project found realisation in a series of buildings which Koenig designed for Christy and Ferrell Burton on the Pacific Coast Highway at Malibu. Although ultimately all one residence, this collection of four buildings offered the clients an affordable solution to their desire. Koenig's plan was to build the units one at a time, allowing the clients to move into the first while the second was under construction and to progressively inhabit the whole as and when their finances allowed. As at the Iwata House and Case Study House #22 Koenig did not cut-and-fill the sloping site but, by raising the buildings above the ground, left the landscape largely undisturbed. To achieve this he used long timber poles set on concrete caissons and these gave their name to the building.

Local building restrictions proscribed the use of steel and, even had it been allowed, the proximity of the buildings to the ocean might have made the choice appear unwise. The technology which Koenig employed to construct the timber frame was, nevertheless, analogous to what he used with steel. Rather like the top floor of the Iwata House, each of the four houses was supported in space by a series of H-frames, the paired cross-beams of which spanned between two parallel rows of poles. These poles were connected linearly by deep beams which, as at the Oberman House, appeared rather like friezes, running the length of the buildings at eaves level. Although linked laterally by walkways and bridges, the units were mono-directional, as at the Chemehuevi project, their side walls were left blank, and balconies projected from the open end outward towards the ocean. But the structural dynamics of timber are not those of steel, and in the absence of welded moment connections, which would have resisted

he poles are erected and the house is under onstruction.

seismic forces as well as stopping the building twisting, diagonal wire bracing was inserted between the poles and below the living decks.

The four houses were arranged in a staggered line, the two outer units containing sleeping accommodation and the two central ones living and work spaces. These were the first to be built. The units themselves are set at different heights, the walkways which connect them stepping up and down to accommodate the changes of level. Thus there is a sense of an undulating landscape, or perhaps a tree house, throughout the whole complex. Whatever the metaphor, one is about as disengaged from the site as in the projecting spaces of Case Study House #22.

1983·Gantert House

6431 La Punta Drive, Los Angeles, California

Perspective drawing of an earlier design, before a window was added to the west elevation.

The house which Koenig built for Michael Gantert in 1983 was arranged, like the earlier Beagles House, with 'an inverted plan'. But now the entrance and living accommodation was retained at the top level, that of the driveway, with the sleeping accommodation set one floor below. Furthermore, by perching the building on the edge of an escarpment, Koenig took advantage of the benefits of structural framing as he had done previously with the Iwata House and the Burton Pole-House.

At the Gantert House, Koenig treated the cross-section with greater sophistication than he had done at the Beagles House, allowing it to read more clearly and thus demonstrate the sense of disengagement between the house and its site. This was achieved by adopting a strongly axial plan and projecting the living spaces out from the hillside while stripping away the side wall to the south so as to leave the accommodation exposed. By contrast, the terminal elevation to the west was left almost blank except for a centrally-placed window at the upper level which accentuated the sense of projection by allowing the central axis to shoot out into space. This axial line was picked up by the open lattice-work of the raised clerestory which provided a further reminder of the skeletal nature of the building.

The structure of the Gantert House is a double cantilever projecting from a central core of four columns supported on concrete caissons driven deep into the hillside. At the upper level, the floor plate, including the carport, measures 36×45 feet but at the lower level it is reduced to 36×35 feet. Not all this was enclosed, for beneath the carport an open deck provided, in close proximity to the bedrooms, outdoor space and a jacuzzi. A grid of 18-inch I-section beams cantilevered from the four 12×8-inch H-section columns support these platforms. On the lowest part of the slope, beneath the bedroom floor plate, is the boiler room which, enclosed in a chain-link fence, recedes into the darkness of the undercroft.

The difficulties of the site necessitated a fresh approach to construction. The steel frame, once erected, became its own scaffolding and the house was assembled with prefabricated components from within this framework. Long-span steel decking clad the roof with shorter-span sheets being used vertically for the walls. The south-facing façade, with views towards downtown Hollywood and the Capital Records tower, was fully glazed, with the glass sliders set back deep within the balconies which sheltered them from solar gain. The single, fixed-light window beneath the clerestory on the west wall looked out towards the Hollywood Bowl while those on the north wall, lighting the dining room, kitchen and laundry, and the bedrooms below, faced the next property.

Internally, the finishes belonged to Koenig's familiar palette, gypsum plaster-board on the walls and boarded or glazed ceiling panels, as at the Oberman House, set within the ribs of the roofing deck. The sense of exposure which the unveiled cross-section provided was continued in the interior, where the lattice beams of the clerestory and the open balustrade of the stair below suggested a fragility which the precarious nature of the site did nothing to dispel. It was not a house for the faint-hearted.

Opposite page:
Perched high above the 101 Freeway, the house enjoys views across downtown Hollywood.

The house cantilevers over the valley below with access at the upper level.

Gantert was a general contractor and it had always been his intention to build the house as a speculation for resale. Consequently, in May 1986, it was on the market for $345,000 and six months later it was in escrow, prior to the completion of the sale, for $298,000. In February 1989 the house was once more on the market with an asking price of $475,000.

After twenty years and a number of different owners the house had suffered a little. Solar panels had been added to the roof and many of the surfaces were damaged or worn and in need of replacement. In 2003 the new owner, Billy Rose of Billy Rose Design & Development, approached Koenig with the intention of remodelling the house and returning it to its former splendour. It was a project which was to extend into 2005, when the house went onto the market again, this time for $1,750,000. Whereas much of the work was cosmetic, metal handrails, for instance, replacing the wooden ones around the stairs and black slate replacing the timber boards of the external deck, there were a number of internal modifications which changed the nature of the building. At the upper level, the kitchen and dining room were opened up to form one space, the tall cabinets which constricted the dining room and separated the kitchen work area from the stairs being removed and replaced with a lower work surface. To allow this, the refrigerator was inserted into the small laundry room which

The upper-floor entrance, with the kitchen to the right and the living area to the left

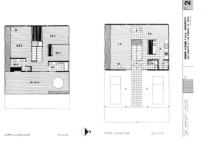

Plans of the house before restoration

Below:
While under construction, the fragility of the structure becomes apparent.

in turn was reduced in size and made contiguous with the adjacent toilet. Downstairs, the jacuzzi was removed and part of the open deck beneath the carport enclosed to provide a new bathroom and a dressing room for the master bedroom, while the two guest bedrooms and the bathroom which ran along the north wall were rearranged and enlarged. All this, of course, was something which the steel-framed structure could accommodate without disturbance, even if the sense of openness which the lower deck had offered was compromised. More concerning, however, particularly for Koenig, was the plan to insert into the blank west wall a 5-foot-wide floor-to-ceiling window for the guest bedroom. He objected to it on the grounds of solar gain, expense and the dangerous nature of the work. But it was done, nevertheless. The result confirms what were perhaps Koenig's worst fears: it really rather destroys the west elevation.

1985·Koenig House #2
12221 Dorothy Street, Los Angeles, California

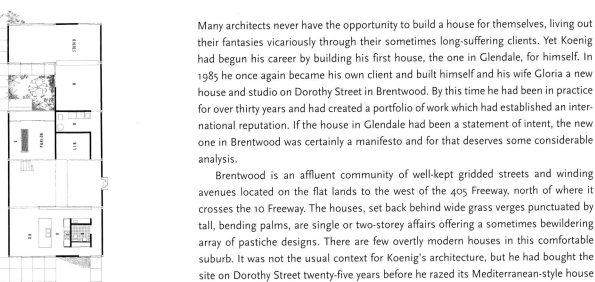

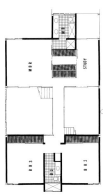

Many architects never have the opportunity to build a house for themselves, living out their fantasies vicariously through their sometimes long-suffering clients. Yet Koenig had begun his career by building his first house, the one in Glendale, for himself. In 1985 he once again became his own client and built himself and his wife Gloria a new house and studio on Dorothy Street in Brentwood. By this time he had been in practice for over thirty years and had created a portfolio of work which had established an international reputation. If the house in Glendale had been a statement of intent, the new one in Brentwood was certainly a manifesto and for that deserves some considerable analysis.

Brentwood is an affluent community of well-kept gridded streets and winding avenues located on the flat lands to the west of the 405 Freeway, north of where it crosses the 10 Freeway. The houses, set back behind wide grass verges punctuated by tall, bending palms, are single or two-storey affairs offering a sometimes bewildering array of pastiche designs. There are few overtly modern houses in this comfortable suburb. It was not the usual context for Koenig's architecture, but he had bought the site on Dorothy Street twenty-five years before he razed its Mediterranean-style house and started again.

The site was long and thin, measuring 40 feet by 120 feet and squeezed in between adjacent properties. The street ran along the south-east front and an access alley along the north west. Thus it offered, despite its restrictions, perhaps the best orientation for which Koenig could hope. Since side views were almost impossible, the house had to open towards the street, or, less agreeably, the alley at the rear. This alignment would provide a warming morning sun but also guarantee shelter as the sun moved higher into the sky. Therefore, if Koenig was to use the site effectively, he had to allow light to penetrate deep into its heart from the street frontage, or borrow it from above the rooftops of the flanking houses without appearing to overshadow them. In the event, he did both. As he said when interviewed, "By taking advantage of a lot of the attributes of the steel, I've been able to build a vertical solution to the problem."

The house is arranged with public pedestrian access from the sidewalk at the front and private vehicular access from the alley at the rear. A low, single-storey studio separates the domestic accommodation from the street. Between the two is a small planted courtyard which acts as a buffer zone. Then the house steps up, first one, then two and finally three storeys of steel frame and glass before dropping off more abruptly to a small rear garden and the carport beyond. To effect a degree of separation, and allow for access, Koenig pulled the side walls in 5 feet or so from the boundary line, thus allowing, on one side, an access route from the street-front entrance to the carport at the rear while, on the other, maintaining an airspace for his wind-door which was fundamental to the design. The other principal circulation route was internal, running from the carport and rear garden, past the drinks bar and through the living room to terminate in the office archive which flanks the planted courtyard outside the studio. Elsewhere, the spaces flowed into each other, separated by low counters and frosted

Ground and upper floor plans

Opposite page:
The triple-height central living space

Delivery of the prefabricated frame

The house under construction, viewed from the street

glass screens, and defined by changes in ceiling height or by the internal bridge and the stairs.

If Koenig had been exploratory in his strategy when building the first house in Glendale, the new house exemplified a thorough understanding of the process. The design was based upon a series of 30-foot steel bents made from 12-inch I-section beams and 6-inch square columns. Set on concrete pads, they marched along the site with relentless authority. At first it appeared complicated and, to help the contractor understand the construction process, Koenig produced a nine-panel step-by-step instruction drawing which encouraged the contractor to reduce the cost by $10,000, for to him time was money and uncertainty suggested delay. Thus, in a single day, the frame was erected, a crane swinging the parts into place and moment connections providing the necessary rigidity to meet seismic design requirements. Then the ground beams and concrete slab were poured.

The street-front entrance, with the office in the foreground and the house rising behind

The house, as it emerged, revolved around a 30-foot three-storey central atrium which acted as both the main living space and the vertical circulation core. On one side, at ground level, were the kitchen and dining area, with a guest toilet, and on the other, flanking the entrance, were the parlour and the music room with the utility room beyond. When the frosted glass panels are withdrawn, the music room, like the kitchen opposite, becomes part of the main living space. Asked by Steve Roden if his house was set up for acoustics or for listening comfort, he replied, "I am not so interested in acoustics, but the ideal listening space is set up for listening as an activity ... My house is designed with music in mind. Besides the music room, which holds all my records and equipment (I have tube amps), the space is calculated for sound. First, the ceiling height is set at a height that breaks up most middle frequencies and has an absorbent pattern. Second, there are spaces on both sides of the three-storey atrium that absorb sound. I have a live space without any reflection at all." When the California EAR Unit played in the house, the music was so loud that some parts of the building were vibrating, but there was no reverberation at all. "As for listening comfort," he continued, "I designed the house so I can hear music from any part of the house. With the windows open from the master bedroom to the atrium, I can hear all the notes. If I open the sliding doors I can hear when outside."

The middle level of the atrium is flanked, on one side, by two guest bedrooms and a bathroom and, on the other, by the master bedroom suite and a study off which there is a balcony. The open-tread stairs rises from below to the bridge that links the two sleeping areas, and then up again to the clerestory level where it gives access to the roof. Here windows surround the whole space and when open provide an exhaust route for the hot air driven up by the ingress of fresh air from the wind-door adjacent to the music room below. This was an experiment, Koenig explained when interviewed, which proved to be almost too efficient: "The wind-door over here" he said, gesturing towards the corner of the room, "which is designed to collect and bring in, introduce ocean breezes over the house is so effective that one can really get chilled by it in the summer time, which I really didn't need to open the whole door to do. I could have done it with a smaller opening. But I wasn't sure." And if there is no wind, the large fans on the atrium ceiling will draw the hot air away all the same.

The range of both materials and colour which Koenig used in the house was limited. The steel frame, where left exposed, was painted white. The cladding was not the familiar T-section roofing deck, but standing-seam sheet-aluminium. "I'm always trying new materials," he continued, "and the latest material for roofing is the standing-seam system, the standing-seam steel roof deck. I used to use the roof deck with the exposed side down. This is similar but with the exposed side up. Now, this is to provide a long-lasting endurable surface for the top."

Aluminium was used for the window frames and again, in polished strips, for the acoustic ceiling of the central atrium. Clear or frosted glass panels separated this volume from the adjacent rooms as well as substituting for balusters on the stairs and bridge, thus allowing as great a sense of reflective transparency as possible. The tiled floor of the atrium is white and is separated from the white plastered walls by a shadow-line, a recessed skirting or kicking board painted black. Thus the sense of modular construction remains, each part a clearly defined component. And throughout the central space the steel frame stands out clearly, sub-dividing the panelled walls both vertically and horizontally to define spaces and levels, while at the same time dropping down below the ceiling plane, to provide a feeling of containment for the otherwise open kitchen and dining area where three grey island units with brushed aluminium trim set out the space.

At first glance the central atrium might seem stark and rather cold. But as the light changes, so does its character. Accents of colour come with the furniture—the chairs are by Eames or Bertoia—or with the free-standing laminated acrylic sculpture by Vasa Mihich. There are no pictures to illustrate the volume but just sounds. "You may have noticed my taste in music is freer than in my architecture," Koenig to Roden. "I believe this is correct (for me) as architecture and painting are permanent (almost) while music is transitional ... Thus I can let sounds go racing by, leaving me to decide what value they may have. If I don't like a particular piece of music I just don't play it again, while a picture on the wall, for example, is stuck there for a long time, whether I like it or not. I could change it, but that's a lot of trouble."

Aerial perspective of the house, showing earlier window arrangements, with sun angle diagrams

The atrium and kitchen beyond, seen from the master bedroom

The dining area and kitchen, with the rear garden beyond

The house on Dorothy Street was in many ways a departure as much as an experiment for Koenig. Rather than have a dramatic or 'unbuildable' site to deal with, he had a standard city plot which challenged him all the more. This he explained when interviewed: "We used to use the horizontal approach to housing when there was a lot of land and now we're kind of pushing it and going up." No longer was the solution the low pavilion or the suspended box, but a three-dimensional assembly of volumes. The environmental innovations such as the wind-door and the controlled reverberation time within the atrium proved surprisingly successful. "As a matter of fact I'm so conservative," he continued, "that many of the things I was worried about would work have worked so well that I really didn't need to go that far in order to solve the problem ... I've produced a different kind of a building. And maybe they don't look that different to a lot of people, but the differences are quite great as time goes on."

1994–1996▸Schwartz House

444 Sycamore Road, Los Angeles, California

In building his own house in Brentwood, Koenig recognised and exploited the opportunities of building upwards which small suburban sites provided. When talking about that house, he observed when interviewed, "I'm looking forward to going even higher than this on my next job." The next job was the house he built in Pacific Palisades, Los Angeles, for Martin Schwartz and his wife.

At first glance the Schwartz house appears to be a rather curious structure, uncertain in its domestic imagery. Robustly metallic, it is a silver cube turned or twisted within a black steel frame. Yet exactly the same observations could have been made thirty-five years earlier about the designs for the Case Study Houses, which might have been mistaken, by the uninformed, for petrol filling stations were it not that their locations made this unlikely. Thus to understand the Schwartz house, it is necessary to investigate the architectural intentions.

The site for this house was a small plot of land on the sloping south-east side of Chautuaqua Canyon, a narrow, wooded valley which runs inland from the ocean and the Pacific Coast Highway to the west. And it is this position and topography which determined the form of the house. Firstly, to achieve adequate floorspace, Koenig had to raise the house by one storey, allowing the sloping land to flow under the site while at the same time releasing enough space for a double garage. This accounted for the frame. Secondly, in order to achieve views down the canyon and to capture the cooling ocean breezes as well as, in winter, the late afternoon sun, he had to set the building askew to the line of the street. So the house was turned 30 degrees within its frame.

By this simple manipulation Koenig suddenly freed up the restrictions which a square plan set in line with the street would have implied. The rotation of the house plan on top of the frame plan exposed residual spaces around each column which were adopted, in one corner, for the spiral stairs and in the opposite corner for a deck and balcony above. Access now need be neither straight to the front or, at right angles, to the side but could be achieved tangentially where the corner of the cube pushed out from within the frame. Beneath the cube, Koenig nestled the nose of the garage, the roof of which became a terrace or patio, and beyond that, in the undercroft, he slipped in the utility room. In 1996, a further bedroom and bathroom were added within this space. Here any sense of basement is quickly dispelled by the fully glazed wall, which can be withdrawn to open the new bedroom to the garden outside.

In contrast to his other houses, the exposed steel frame at the Schwartz house offers no guide to the arrangement of the interior spaces. Indeed, it is quite detached from them. Instead, there is a secondary frame which forms the cube comprising deep I-section beams and peristylar square-section columns. Thus the interior space is left completely free of structural elements. This allowed Koenig to place the kitchen/bathroom core off-centre and to the rear, allowing space for the entrance hallway to one side and for kitchen activities to the other. This larger area was separated from the dining area, as in his own house, by the grey kitchen work surface with brushed aluminium trim. The lowered ceiling and tiled floor clearly defined the zone.

The entranceway to the house

The living and dining area took up the whole frontage of the house and opened, through glass sliders, onto the triangular deck which led in turn down to the roof terrace above the garage. With the exception of the hardwood floor, Koenig treated the space in the same way as he had done his own house, the white steel frame standing out, as in relief, against the white panels of the wall and the black shadow line where the wall met the floor.

The upper floor was arranged similarly, but with the double bathroom core slid slightly to one corner to allow space for three bedrooms and adjacent closet space. Here the difficulties of a square plan become apparent, for to give access to the rooms, a corridor has to wrap around three sides of the bathroom core, although economy is achieved by incorporating one of these as a closet area within the master bedroom

While the frame aligns with the site, the house turns to take advantage of the location.

suite. Had the stairs been placed centrally on plan this arrangement might have been avoided, but as it is, the stairs protrude in a glazed tower to the rear, the yellow open-tread steps cantilevering from one circular corner column of the external frame. It is an alerting if quixotic gesture at odds with the rest of the building.

The stair treads provide the only touch of colour in the house, apart from the furnishings and the hardwood floor. The exterior is clad with ribbed aluminium roof decking applied in unbroken vertical sheets, and all exposed steelwork is painted black. Against this, the aluminium framing for the windows and the frosted-glass panels surrounding the balconies and roof terrace stand out as sharp rectangles. The concrete blockwork of the garage below is left unadorned and the street-front clad again with profiled metal sheeting beneath a slender, black open-web beam. Here the imagery is

noticeably industrial, but just one glance across the street at the black steel mail box which Koenig placed in a row of common-or-garden curb-side letter drops, should alert the unwary to expect something different.

The dining area with the kitchen, below a lowered ceiling, beyond

first and second floor plan

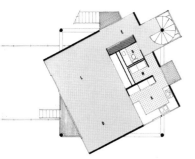

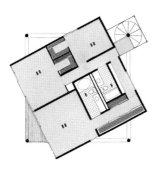

Life and Work

Opposite page:
Pierre Koenig on site

Right:
Young Pierre Koenig at the beach in California

1925 ► 17 October, Pierre Francis Koenig born in San Francisco, California

1939 ► Moved with family to Los Angeles, California

1943 ► Attended School of Engineering, University of Utah, Salt Lake City, Utah

1943–1946 ► Flash Ranger Observer, US Army

1946–1948 ► Attended Pasadena City College, Pasadena, California

1948–1952 ► Attended Department of Architecture, University of Southern California, Los Angeles, California

1950 ► Worked for Raphael Soriano.
Koenig House #1, Glendale, California

1952 ► 2 August, Graduated as Bachelor of Architecture, University of Southern California, Los Angeles, California
Set up private practice

1953 ► Married Merry Thompson; one child, Randall Francis Koenig, in 1954
Lamel House, Glendale, California
Squire House, La Cañada, California
Scott House, Tujunga, California

1956 ► Worked for Jones and Emmons

1957 ► 2 October, passed California State Board of Examiners Licensing Exams in Architecture
23 December, elected member of the American Istitute of Architects (AIA)
São Paolo Bienale IV Exhibition Award (First Prize), São Paolo, Brazil
AIA-*House and Home* magazine Award
Architectural League of New York Award
Burwash House, Tujunga, California

1958 ► 11 February, elected member of the AIA Southern California Chapter
Divorced Merry Thompson
Radio Station KYOR, Blythe, California

Metcalf House, Los Angeles, California
Bailey House (Case Study House #21), Los Angeles, California

1959 ► AIA-*Sunset* magazine Honor Award
Western Construction magazine Honor Award

1960 ► AIA-*House and Home* magazine Award
Married Gaile Carson; one child, Jean Pierre Koenig, in 1961
Stahl House (Case Study House #22), Los Angeles, California
Seidel House, Los Angeles, California

1961 ► Joined the Department of Architecture, University of Southern California, Los Angeles, California
Seidel Beach House, Malibu, California
Willheim House, Los Angeles, California
Prefabricated Houses, St Jean, Quebec, Canada

1961–1962 ► AIA-*Sunset* magazine Award

1962 ► AIA-*House and Home* magazine Award
Johnson House, Carmel Valley, California
Oberman House, Palos Verdes, California

Pierre Koenig, a flash ranger in the US Army

Bethlehem Steel Company Travelling Exhibition Pavilion

1963 ▸ AIA-*House and Home* magazine Award
American Institute of Iron and Steel Award
Iwata House, Monterey Park, California
Mosque (project), Los Angeles, California
Beagles House, Los Angeles, California

1964 ▸ Appointed Assistant Professor, Department of Architecture, University of Southern California, Los Angeles, California
Best Exhibition Building Award, Portland, Oregon

1966
Electronic Enclosures Incorporated Factory and Showroom, El Segundo, California

1967 ▸ AIA Southern California Chapter Architectural Grand Prix for 36 Best Buildings in Los Angeles since 1947

1968 ▸ Appointed Associate Professor, Department of Architecture, University of Southern California, Los Angeles, California, and granted tenure

1970
West House, Vallejo, California

1971 ▸ Elected to College of Fellows of the AIA

1971–1976
Chemehuevi Prefabricated Housing Tract, Lake Havasu, California

Pierre Koenig at an exhibition of his work

Pierre and Gloria Koenig

1973
Franklyn Medical Building, West Hollywood, California

1975 ▸ Divorced Gaile Carson

1979
Burton Pole-House, Malibu, California

1981
Zapata Restaurant and Disco (Franklyn Dinner Club), Thousand Oaks, California

1983 ▸ AIA 200/2000 Award
Gantert House, Los Angeles, California

1984 ▸ AIA Olympic Architect Award
Rollé addition #1 (Seidel House), Los Angeles, California
Stuermer House, Oahu, Hawaii

1985 ▸ Married Gloria Kaufman; two stepsons, Thomas and Barry Kaufman
Koenig House #2, Los Angeles, California

1989 ▸ Los Angeles Department of Cultural Affairs Award.

1989–1990 ▸ Case Study House #22, MOCA Exhibit, Los Angeles, California

1994
Rollé addition #2 (Seidel House), Los Angeles, California

1995
Riebe restoration and addition (Johnson House), Carmel Valley, California

1996 ▸ AIA California Council 25 Year Award
AIA California Council Maybeck Award for Lifetime Achievement
Appointed Professor, Department of Architecture, University of Southern California, Los Angeles, California
Schwartz House, Santa Monica, California

1998 ▸ Distinguished Alumni Award, Department of Architecture, University of Southern California, Los Angeles, California

1999 ▸ AIA Los Angeles Chapter Gold Medal
Star of Design for Lifetime Achievement in Architecture, Pacific Design Center, Los Angeles, California
Distinguished Professor of Architecture, University of Southern California, Los Angeles, California

2000 ▸ Elected Honorary Fellow of the Royal Institute of British Architects
City of Los Angeles Historic Preservation 2000 Award of Excellence
Los Angeles Conservancy Preservation Award 2000
Pasadena City College Distinguished Alumni Award
Gold Medal Lifetime Achievement Award, Tau Sigma Delta Society of Architects and Landscape Architects

2001 ▸ National Design Award, Architecture Design Finalist, Smithsonian/Cooper-Hewitt National Design Museum
AIA California Council 25 Year Award
Ressner modular addition, Brentwood, California

2002
Koppany Pool House, Los Angeles, California

2003
LaFetra House, Malibu, California
Tarassoly & Mehran House, Malibu, California
Winters House, Dallas, Texas

2004 ▸ 4 April, died at home, Los Angeles, California

Map

Glendale
Koenig House #1
Lamel House

Los Angeles
Bailey House (CSH #21)
Beagles House
Gantert House
Koenig House #2
Schwartz House
Seidel House
Stahl House (CSH #22)

Malibu
Burton Pole-House

Monterey Park
Iwata House

Palos Verdes
Oberman House

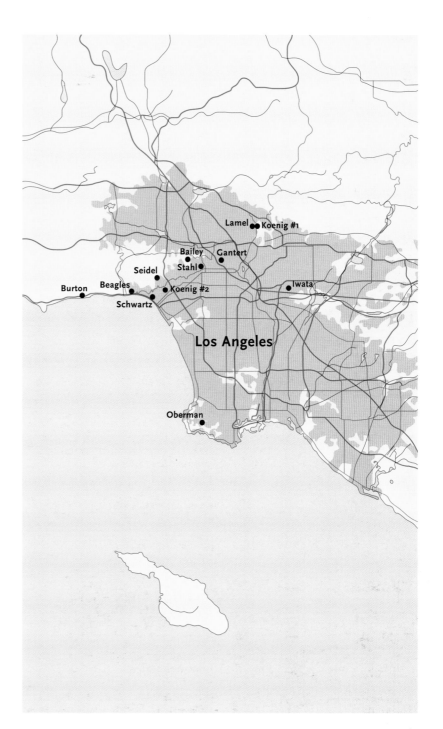

Bibliography

▶ Anon, 'Small House by Pierre Koenig, Designer', *Arts & Architecture*, January 1954
▶ Anon, 'Steel Frame House', *Arts & Architecture*, June 1955
▶ Anon, 'An Economical House Results from an Adventurous Spirit', *Living For Young Homemakers*, February 1956
▶ Anon, 'Jeunes architectes dans le monde', *L'Architecture d'aujourd'hui*, September 1957
▶ Anon, 'Framed and roofed ... in 2 days', *Sunset, the Magazine of Western Living*, April 1959
▶ Alison Arieff and Bryan Burkhart, *Pre Fab*, Gibbs Smith, Utah, 2000
▶ Eryn Brown, 'A Case Study in Stewardship,' *Los Angeles Times*, 4 August 2005
▶ Peggy Cochran, *Koenig*, St. James Press, Andover/Detroit, 1988
▶ Barbara East, 'There May Be a Steel House ... In Your Very Near Future', *San Francisco Examiner, Modern Living*, 18 September 1955
▶ David Hay, 'Returning to the Scene', *House Beautiful*, October 1998
▶ Pierre Koenig, *Johnson House*, written description, unpublished mss., no date
▶ Pierre Koenig, 'Low-Cost Production House', *Arts & Architecture*, March 1957
▶ Pierre Koenig, 'Modern Production House', *Arts & Architecture*, January 1961
▶ Brandon LaBelle and Steve Roden, *Site of Sound: of Architecture & the Ear*, Errant Bodies Press, Los Angeles, 1999
▶ Esther McCoy, 'Steel around the Pacific', *Los Angeles Examiner, Pictorial Living*, 25 February 1956
▶ Esther McCoy, 'What I Believe ... A statement of architectural principles by Pierre Koenig', *Los Angeles Times Home Magazine*, 21 July 1957
▶ National Steel Corporation, 'I built this house of steel for many reasons ... ', *Time*, 9 April 1956, and *Newsweek*, 16 April 1956
▶ Christopher Reed, 'Pierre Koenig', *The Independent*, 2004
▶ Elizabeth Smith A. T., *Case Study Houses*, Taschen, Cologne, 2006
▶ Elizabeth Smith A. T., *Case Study Houses. The Complete CSH Program 1945–1966*, Taschen, Cologne, 2002
▶ James Steele and David Jenkins, *Pierre Koenig*, Phaidon Press, London, 1998
▶ Margaret Stovall, 'Home of the Week', *Independent Star-News*, 31 August 1958

Acknowledgements

I am particularly grateful for the guidance and assistance given to me by Gloria Koenig and by Jan Ipach, and to all those owners of a Koenig house who, over the years, have shown me their homes or talked so enthusiastically about them. Without their help, this book could not have been written.

The Author

Neil Jackson is a British architect and architectural historian who has written extensively on modern architecture in California, where he taught between 1985 and 1990. His 2002 book *Graig Ellwood* won the Sir Banister Fletcher Award in 2003. This study of Pierre Koenig is the result of a long friendship and a mark of respect for a great architect. Professor Jackson currently teaches at the University of Liverpool.

Credits